VC

OF THE

SECOND WORLD WAR

VCs

OF THE

SECOND WORLD WAR

TEN STORIES OF BRAVERY AND COURAGE

STEPHEN WYNN

Pen & Sword

MILITARY

AN IMPRINT OF PEN & SWORD BOOKS LTD.
YORKSHIRE ~ PHILADELPHIA

First published in Great Britain in 2020 by
Pen & Sword MILITARY
An imprint of Pen & Sword Books Ltd
Yorkshire – Philadelphia

Typeset in Times New Roman 11.5/14 by Aura Technology and Software Services,
India
Printed and bound in 4Edge Ltd, Essex, SS5 4AD

Pen & Sword Books Limited incorporates the imprints of Atlas, Archaeology,
Aviation, Discovery, Family History, Fiction, History, Maritime, Military, Military
Classics, Politics, Select, Transport, True Crime, Air World, Frontline Publishing, Leo
Cooper, Remember When, Seaforth Publishing, The Praetorian Press, Wharncliffe
Local History, Wharncliffe Transport, Wharncliffe True Crime and White Owl.

For a complete list of Pen & Sword titles please contact
PEN & SWORD BOOKS LIMITED
47 Church Street, Barnsley, South Yorkshire, S70 2AS, England
E-mail: enquiries@pen-and-sword.co.uk • Website: www.pen-and-sword.co.uk
Or
PEN AND SWORD BOOKS
1950 Lawrence Rd, Havertown, PA 19083, USA
E-mail: Uspen-and-sword@casematepublishers.com
Website: www.penandswordbooks.com

Contents

Introduction

The Victoria Cross is the highest award for valour 'in the face of the enemy', available to all ranks and to all branches of British and Commonwealth military forces. It may also be awarded to civilians acting under military command. It was officially introduced by Her Majesty Queen Victoria on 29 January 1856, when she issued a warrant announcing its institution, backdated to 1854, to include acts of valour during the Crimean War. Its arrival was announced in the *London Gazette* on 5 February 1856.

Queen Victoria had instructed the War Office to create a new medal that would recognise neither a man's birth nor class. The medal was meant to be a simple decoration, one that was highly prized and eagerly sought after by those in the military services. To keep it simple, Queen Victoria, with some support from her husband, Prince Albert, made clear her views that she did not like the suggestion that the new award should be called *The Military Order of Victoria*. Instead she suggested that the award should be named the *Victoria Cross*. Nobody disagreed with the queen's suggestion, and so it was that the Victoria Cross came into being.

How does the process work? A recommendation for an individual to be awarded the Victoria Cross is usually made by an officer of the regiment the individual concerned was serving with at the time he displayed his act of bravery. Any such recommendation requires the support of three witnesses, although this can be more. There have been occasions where this part of the process has not been adhered to. The recommendation has to pass through different levels of military inspection by senior military figures and committees, before it is placed before the Secretary of State for Defence. If it receives approval at this level the recommendation is then placed before the monarch who approves the award with her or his signature. The award is announced in the *London Gazette* and includes a detailed citation for the action that led to the award. The award of almost every single Victoria

Cross has always been announced in this same way. The only exception was the award of the Victoria Cross to the American Unknown Soldier in 1921.

The warrant for the Victoria Cross does not include a specific provision in relation to who should actually present the award to the recipient, but during Queen Victoria's reign, when a total of 472 were awarded, she personally presented 185 of them.

The first awards ceremony, which was also the largest for the issue of the Victoria Cross, took place at Hyde Park in London on a sunny 26 June 1857, when Queen Victoria handed out 62 of the 111 that had been awarded to recipients who had carried out acts of valour whilst serving during the Crimean War.

It was a unique occasion in that it was the first such award that made no distinction between officers and enlisted men and it is estimated that there was a crowd of some 100,000 people who had turned up for the occasion. There was also a strong military presence of some 4,000 men from the Life Guards, the Cavalry, the Royal Navy, the Royal Artillery, and infantry from the Rifle Brigade and the Foot Guards.

At the allotted time, the queen gracefully leant down from her horse and placed the award on the chest of each of the men as they were led up to her in turn. The prince consort, who was seated upon his fine steed, to the right of the queen, bowed to each of them as a mark of respect for their individual acts of bravery.

Charles Davis Lucas, from County Monaghan in Ireland, was the fourth to receive his award from the queen that day. He had joined the Navy as a 13-year-old boy, and during the Crimean War was a crew member of HMS *Hecla*, part of an Anglo-French fleet who were at the eastern end of the Baltic Sea, bombarding the Russian fortress of Bomarsund. It was a formidable structure which had eighty massive guns to defend itself with. As the *Hecla* drew closer, a live shell fired from the fortress landed on the ship's deck and lay there like a ticking time bomb, only a matter of time before it exploded. If it had done, great damage would have been caused to the ship, and many of the crew would have undoubtedly died. Lucas, a young man, 20 years old at the time, was coolness personified, way beyond his years. He picked up the live shell, holding it in both arms, conscious it could explode at any second, carefully made his way to the side of the ship and dropped it into the sea, where it exploded soon after with a terrific bang, sending a giant plume of water into the air and down on to the deck.

For his actions of selfless bravery, Lucas was immediately promoted to the rank of lieutenant. His was the first act of valour deemed to be worthy of the award of the Victoria Cross, ensuring that Lucas would go down in history for two reasons.

He spent the rest of his long military career serving in the Royal Navy. Before he retired in 1914, he had risen to the rank of rear admiral, and died at Tunbridge Wells in Kent at the age of 80.

Over the years, the Victoria Cross has also been awarded by other senior members of the Royal family, or by civil or military dignitaries. Some lesser-ranking medals have even been sent to the next of kin through the post, when awards have been awarded posthumously. Strangely enough, when the Royal Warrant for the Victoria Cross was first drawn up, no allowance had been made for it to be awarded posthumously, even though the standard for being awarded the Victoria Cross was so high that being killed in the very act of winning the award was not unusual.

Whether the initial omission of such a clause was simply an oversight on the part of the authorities, or had been a consideration but was then dismissed because nobody could see the point in giving such an award to somebody who was dead, is unclear. Between 1857 and 1899, which was the period of time between the Indian Mutiny and the beginning of the Second Boer War, the *London Gazette* included six names with a note explaining that they would have been awarded the Victoria Cross for their acts of bravery had they survived their ordeal. Between September 1900 and April 1901 a further three names appeared in the *London Gazette* for gallantry, which had similar notes attached to them. But it was the Boer War that eventually changed matters when it came to the awarding of the Victoria Cross, as six such awards were made posthumously. This included the three men mentioned above between 1900 and 1901, and three others, the awards finally appearing in the *London Gazette* on 8 August 1902, making them the first official posthumous awards.

The six men were;

> Trooper Herman Albrecht, killed in action on 6 January 1900.
>
> Lieutenant Robert Digby-Jones, killed in action on 6 January 1900.

INTRODUCTION

Sergeant Alfred Atkinson, died of wounds on 21 February 1900.

Captain David Younger, died of wounds on 11 July 1900.

Private John Barry, killed in action on 8 January 1901.

Lieutenant Gustavus Coulson, died of wounds on 18 May 1901.

In 1907, the policy in relation to posthumous awards for earlier wars was reversed and a further six officers and men, dating back to the Indian Mutiny, had Victoria Crosses sent to their immediate next of kin. The names of each of these individuals were subsequently mentioned in the *London Gazette*.

The Royal Warrant for the Victoria Cross was not actually amended to allow for posthumous awards until 1920, despite the fact that a quarter of all awards of the Victoria Cross during the First World War were made posthumously. The 1920 Royal Warrant, also for the first time opened up the Victoria Cross to be awarded to women, but to date no woman has ever been awarded it.

Although the Victoria Cross is available to military forces from any Commonwealth nation, most now have their own individual honours system and their own version of the Victoria Cross. Canada began the trend more than fifty years ago, in 1967, and others subsequently followed. Canada called its version the Canadian Victoria Cross, whereas in Australia it is the Victoria Cross for Australia, and in New Zealand, it is referred to as the Victoria Cross for New Zealand.

Before the Crimean War, Britain did not really have a system in place where men could receive awards for acts of bravery. For anybody in the military during the nineteenth century, it really was a case of 'us' and 'them', as any kind of award for bravery tended to be kept back for officers. For those men it usually meant they could be put forward for the Order of the Bath; be given a brevet promotion; or for what were deemed to be lesser acts of bravery, a Mention in Despatches. The reason why such awards were usually the sole domain of officers was because commanding officers in the field usually only watched what their junior officers were doing and had no time for men from the other ranks. This meant that the soldiers doing the actual physical fighting more often than not saw their acts of bravery go totally unnoticed. Snobbery was just as rife in the army as it was in society as a whole.

Other nations, such as France and Holland, had awards for valour and bravery that were all inclusive and did not discriminate against a man based on his class in society or his army rank. These awards were the Legion d'honneur in France, in place since 1802, and the Order of William, first established in Holland in 1815. It was another forty-two years before the first Victoria Cross was awarded.

Hancocks jewellers of London, who were established on 1 January 1849, by Charles Hancock, have been responsible for producing every Victoria Cross ever made.

The only point of question about the Victoria Cross is the origin of the metal that they were made from. The story has been that the medals are cast from two captured Russian cannon, which were taken at the Siege of Sevastopol, between 17 October 1854 and 9 September 1855. There is also talk that the guns in question are in fact Chinese and not Russian. This may well be the case, as just because they were captured from the Russians at Sevastopol in Russia, doesn't necessarily mean they were of Russian manufacture.

The remaining bronze, whatever its origins, is stored in a secure vault at the Ministry of Defence facility at Donnington, near Telford in Shropshire, also home to elements of the Royal Logistics Corps. It has been estimated that there is only enough metal left from the current source for a maximum of a further eighty-five Victoria Crosses to be cast. The design incorporates a cross that is 36mm in width, which bears the crown of Saint Edward, surmounted by a lion. It includes the inscription: FOR VALOUR. The original choice of words was FOR THE BRAVE, but this was changed on the suggestion of Queen Victoria, because she felt that to keep the original version was inappropriate since it suggested that not all men in battle were brave.

There is also sufficient space on the rear of the suspension bar, which connects the medal to the ribbon, to include the recipient's name, rank, service number and unit. On the reverse side of the medal the date of the act for which the medal was awarded is engraved on a circular panel in its centre.

The original warrant for the Victoria Cross stated that it should consist of a Maltese cross. The fact that it has never been the case has never been corrected on the warrant. Originally the colour of the ribbon was red for the army and blue for the Royal Navy. However, when the Royal Air Force was formed on 1 April 1918, the blue ribbon was no longer used. On 22 May, King George V signed a warrant stating that all further awards of the Victoria Cross would come with a red ribbon, and that all living recipients of the naval version should exchange their original blue ribbon for the red one.

There have been cases where a Victoria Cross has been awarded by the drawing of a ballot. Such a scenario takes place in the case of a gallant and daring act having been performed by a squadron, a ship's company or a detached body of men such as Royal Marines, when all men are deemed equally brave and deserving of the Victoria Cross. The officers select one officer, the NCOs select one individual and the private soldiers or seamen select two individuals. In all, forty-six Victoria Crosses have been awarded in this way, with twenty-nine of these having come about during the time of the Indian Mutiny. A further four awards were granted to Q Battery, Royal Horse Artillery at Korn Spruit on 31 March 1900, during the Second Boer War. The final ballot awards for the army were the six awards to the Lancashire Fusiliers at 'W' Beach during the landings at Gallipoli on 25 April 1915, although somewhat surprisingly, three of these awards did not appear in the *London Gazette* until 1917. The final seven ballot awards were the only naval ballot awards with three awards to two Q Ships in 1917 and four awards for the Zeebrugge Raid in 1918.

Although it is still possible for the Victoria Cross to be awarded by ballot, the Zeebrugge Raid of 1918 remains the last time that such an event took place. This aspect is vastly different to the time between 1858 and 1881, when being awarded the Victoria Cross did not require the action, which resulted in the individual being honoured, to be 'in the face of the enemy'. During those years it could be awarded for actions taken 'under circumstances of extreme danger'. Six were awarded during this time, five of which came from a single incident during what history has recorded as the Expedition to the Andaman Islands in 1867.

On 21 March 1867, the captain and seven crew of the vessel, the *Assam Valley*, went ashore on the island of Little Andaman for wood and were seen to get over the reef at the southern tip of the island by those who had remained behind on the *Assam Valley*. The captain and men brought their boat ashore and went into the jungle. But two days later, when they still had not been heard from, the *Assam Valley*, with its remaining crew, sailed to Rangoon to report the event.

Eventually, and after another attempt at locating the captain and seven men, resulting in members of the rescue party becoming stranded on the beach, the *Assam Valley* returned to the island, and sent a boat ashore to rescue their stranded colleagues. The five men on that boat were: Assistant Surgeon Campbell Mills Douglas, MD, Private Thomas Murphy, Private James Cooper, Private David Bell, and Private William Griffiths. For their actions that day, all five men were awarded the Victoria Cross.

The citation detailing the action, which resulted in their being honoured, appeared in the *London Gazette* on 17 December 1867, was worded as follows:

> The Queen has been graciously pleased to signify Her intention to confer the decoration of the Victoria Cross on the undermentioned Officer and Private Soldiers of Her Majesty's Army, whose claims to the same have been submitted for Her Majesty's approval, for their gallant conduct at the Little Andaman Island, as recorded against their names, viz: 2nd Battalion, 24th Regiment: Assistant-Surgeon Campbell Millis Douglas, M.D, Private Thomas Murphy, Private James Cooper, Private David Bell, Private William Griffiths. For the very gallant and daring manner in which, on the 7th of May, 1867, they risked their lives in manning a boat and proceeding through a dangerous surf to the rescue of some of their comrades, who formed part of an expedition which had been sent to the Island of Little Andaman, by order of the Chief Commissioner of British Burma, with the view of ascertaining the fate of the Commander and seven of the crew of the ship 'Assam Valley,' who had landed there, and were supposed to have been murdered by the natives.

> The officer who commanded the troops on the occasion reports:

> About an hour later in the day Dr Douglas, 2nd Battalion, 24th Regiment, and the four Privates referred to, gallantly manning the second gig, made their way through the surf almost to the shore, but finding their boat was half filled with water, they retired. A second attempt made by Dr Douglas and party proved successful, five of us being safely passed through the surf to the boats outside. A third and last trip got the whole of the party left on shore safe to the boats. It

is stated that Dr Douglas accomplished these trips through the surf to the shore by no ordinary exertion. He stood in the bows of the boat, and worked her in an intrepid and seamanlike manner, cool to a degree, as if what he was then doing was an ordinary act of everyday life. The four Privates behaved in an equally cool and collected manner, rowing through the roughest surf when the slightest hesitation or want of pluck on the part of any one of them would have been attended by the gravest results. It is reported that seventeen officers and men were thus saved from what must otherwise have been a fearful risk, if not certainty of death.

Initially the Victoria Cross wasn't awarded to 'colonial' troops or sailors, only British ones. That changed in 1867 with Major Charles Heaphy who was of the New Zealand army, but acting under the command of British forces during fighting in the New Zealand Wars in 1864.

In late 1864, Major General Thomas Galloway, who was the commander of the New Zealand colonial forces, recommended Major Heaphy for the Victoria Cross for his actions at Paterangi. Galloway's recommendation was supported by Sir George Grey, who was serving a second term as the governor of New Zealand, despite knowing that Heaphy and another man (also recommended for the Victoria Cross for an action earlier in the campaign) were neither in the British army nor navy.

At the time, since only regular British military personnel could be awarded the Victoria Cross, it meant that Heaphy, who was serving as a militiaman, was ineligible for the award. Grey argued that as Heaphy was under the effective command of British officers at the time of his act of bravery, an exception in his case should be made. In London, however, the authorities disagreed with Grey's interpretation, and the recommendation was turned down.

Heaphy refused to accept this response and decided to challenge the decision. With support from Grey, Havelock, and General Duncan Cameron, commander of British forces in New Zealand, his remonstrations eventually bore fruit, and he was finally successful in being awarded the Victoria Cross. On 8 February 1867, Queen Victoria made a declaration that the local forces of New Zealand would be eligible for the award of the Victoria Cross. The very same day, Heaphy's award of the Victoria Cross, the first to a New Zealander and also to a non-regular soldier, appeared in the *London Gazette*. The citation for the award included the following words:

> For his gallant conduct at the skirmish on the banks of the Mangapiko River, in New Zealand, on the 11th of February, 1864, in assisting a wounded soldier of the 40th Regiment, who had fallen into a hollow among the thickest of the concealed Maories. Whilst doing so, he became the target for a volley at a few feet distant. Five balls pierced his clothes and cap, and he was wounded in three places. Although hurt, he continued to aid the wounded until the end of the day. Major Heaphy was at the time in charge of a party of soldiers of the 40th and 50th Regiments, under the orders of Lieutenant Colonel Sir Henry Marshman Havelock, Bart., VC, GCBDL, the Senior Officer on the spot, who had moved rapidly down to the place where the troops were hotly engaged and pressed.

Heaphy was presented with his Victoria Cross at a parade and presentation held at Albert Barracks in Auckland, New Zealand, on 11 May 1867.

The issue of colonial troops once again came to the fore in 1881. This time it was a slightly different point, but the principle was still the same. Surgeon John McCrea, an officer of the South African Forces, was recommended for the Victoria Cross during hostilities, which at the time they took place, did not have the support or the agreement of the British Government. McCrea's recommendation for the Victoria Cross led to the principle being established that gallant conduct could be recognised and rewarded, regardless of any political perspective at the time. An example of this would be the Vietnam War, which Britain was not officially involved in, but that didn't stop four Australian soldiers from being awarded the Victoria Cross, for acts of bravery whilst fighting there.

John Frederick McCrea was 26 years old, and a surgeon in the 1st Cape Mounted Yeomanry, of the South African Forces, with which he was serving during the Transvaal War, when he performed the following actions for which he was awarded the Victoria Cross.

> On 14 January 1881, at Tweefontein, Basutoland, South Africa, the burghers had been forced to retire under a most determined

enemy attack, with a loss of 16 killed and 21 wounded. Surgeon McCrea was the only doctor present and notwithstanding a serious wound on the breast bone, which he dressed himself, he most gallantly took the casualties into shelter and continued to attend to the wounded throughout the day. Had it not been for this devotion to duty on the part of Surgeon McCrea, there would undoubtedly have been much greater suffering and loss of life.

Indian soldiers did not become eligible for the Victoria Cross until 1911. The first two awards to Indian soldiers appeared in the *London Gazette* on 7 December 1914, when Darwan Sing Negi and Khudadad Khan had the citations for the awards of their Victoria Crosses included. Negi was presented with his Victoria Cross on 5 December 1914, by King George V, who was in France visiting troops. This made Negi one of only a few recipients of the Victoria Cross to have physically been presented with their medal, before it was announced in the *London Gazette*.

The reason Indian troops were not originally eligible to be awarded the Victoria Cross was because since 1837 they had been eligible for the Indian Order of Merit, which was the oldest British gallantry award for general issue. The other point worth mentioning is that it was not actually until 1860 that Indian troops came under Crown control. Prior to this, Indian troops were employed by the Honourable East India Company. Any Europeans who served with the Honourable East India Company, either officers or men, were not eligible for the Indian Order of Merit, but they were eligible to be awarded the Victoria Cross from October 1857.

The Victoria Cross is the highest award for valour in the United Kingdom. At an investiture, recipients of the Victoria Cross are always presented with their awards first, even ahead of an individual being awarded a knighthood.

In a row of medals or ribbons, the Victoria Cross is always the first decoration indicated. When in a written format, the letters VC are always the first set of post-nominal letters used to indicate a decoration or order. The George Cross has equal precedence to the Victoria Cross, and is awarded for acts of supreme valour, though not in the face of the enemy. Despite this distinction it is still second to the Victoria Cross in order, simply because it is a newer award.

King Edward VII only gave the Victoria Cross its precedence on a bar brooch in 1902. The cross may also be worn as a miniature decoration on a brooch or a chain with Mess jacket, or a white or black tie function.

Any member of Her Majesty's armed forces, and of any rank, will always salute a recipient of the Victoria Cross, regardless of their rank. This is because of tradition and respect, which in turn gives the gesture value and worth. Individuals do not carry out such a salute because they have to under Queens Regulations and Orders, or because the award's warrant states that they must, but because they want to.

The Victoria Cross has always carried an annuity for those who have earned the right to wear it. In its original form the warrant stated that non-commissioned officers, private soldiers or seamen, whose names were recorded on the Victoria Cross Register, were entitled to a £10 a year annuity. This was altered by Queen Victoria in 1898, when she increased the annual sum to £50 for those, who for whatever reason were unable to earn a living, regardless of whether that was because of old age or infirmity. This amount was increased in 2015 to a tax free amount of £10,000 per annum.

An interesting aspect of the original Royal Warrant for the Victoria Cross is that it allowed for a recipient of the award to have their name removed from the official Victoria Cross register. Such removals were allowed if a recipient was involved in 'certain wholly discreditable circumstances, and his pension cancelled'. Between 1861 and 1908, there were eight recipients of the Victoria Cross who forfeited their awards. Although if so merited the award can be restored, not one of them ever had those awards reinstated or therefore had their names re-entered on to the Victoria Cross register.

This approach was changed on 26 July 1920, when King George V, who felt so strongly about the issue that he stated that no matter what crime a man on whom the Victoria Cross had been conferred had committed, the award should not be forfeited. Even if such a recipient were to be hanged for murder, the man should be allowed to wear his Victoria Cross standing on the scaffold.

There have even been at least two Victoria Crosses that have been awarded to British military personnel, on the strength of evidence provided by enemy officers.

Quite possibly the most unusual, and the least-known-about, awarding of the Victoria Cross took place in 1856, when a Victoria Cross was bestowed upon the Netley Military Hospital near Southampton by Queen Victoria herself. What she actually did was to place a Victoria Cross medal beneath the foundation stone of the hospital. One hundred and ten years later, when the hospital was closed down and demolished in 1966, the Victoria Cross, known as 'The Netley VC', was retrieved. Its new home is the Army Medical Services Museum, at Mytchett, Aldershot. It has never been included in the official list of Victoria Crosses awarded.

By the very nature of the actions that individuals carried out to be awarded a Victoria Cross, they have understandably become very collectable over the years. Since the late 1800s, more than 300 Victoria Crosses have been sold, either by auction or private sales.

According to an article on Wikipedia, the Middlesex Regiment paid a then record sum of £900 in October 1966 for a Victoria Cross that had been won during the Battle of the Somme. There were a total of fifty-one Victoria Crosses awarded during the duration of the battle between 1 July and 18 November 1916, two of which were to men of the 12th Battalion, Middlesex Regiment. Both men were awarded their medals as a result of acts of bravery carried out on 26 September 1916. The two men were Private Frederick Jeremiah Edwards, whose medal is on display at the National Army Museum at Chelsea, and Private Robert Edward Ryder, whose medal is displayed at the Lord Ashcroft Victoria Cross Gallery at the Imperial War Museum. Both men survived the war.

Which of the two medals was originally purchased by the Middlesex Regiment is unclear.

Jump forward forty-three years and Lord Ashcroft, who began his Victoria Cross collection in 1986, purchased the Victoria Cross and bar, won by Noel Chavasse during the First World War, from St Peter's College, Oxford in November 2009. The price he paid was reported to be £1.5 million.

On 23 November 2017, an eleven group medal set which included the Victoria Cross, and a Distinguished Service Order and two bars, awarded during the course of the First World War to Commander, and later Vice Admiral, Gordon Campbell, realised a sale price of £700,000.

Sadly, over the years a number of Victoria Crosses have been stolen. On the evening of 24 December 1978, the Victoria Cross that was awarded to Brigadier Milton Fowler Gregg, when he was a lieutenant serving with the Royal Canadian Regiment during the First World War, was stolen from the Royal Canadian Regiment Museum in London, Ontario. The medal has never been recovered.

In 1973, the Victoria Cross awarded to Russian-born, Canadian Corporal, Filip Konowal, was also stolen from the same Royal Canadian Museum. It was returned to the museum again on 23 August 2004, after it was offered for sale by an antique shop to the Jeffrey Hoare Auction House in London, Ontario.

Charles Upham's Victoria Cross and bar were amongst more than one hundred medals stolen from the Queen Elizabeth II Army Memorial Museum in Waiouru, New Zealand, on 2 December 2007. The New Zealand Police announced that all the medals had been recovered, and returned to the museum on 16 February 2008.

This part of the book would not be complete without mentioning the remarkable story of Mrs Elizabeth Webber Harris, who with the permission of Queen Victoria, was allowed to be presented with a gold replica of the Victoria Cross in 1869. On 22 February 1859 she married Webber Desborough Harris, who at the time was a captain with the 2nd Bengal Fusiliers. In May 1861 it was renamed the 1st Royal Bengal Fusiliers, and on its transfer into the British army in September 1862 it became the 104th Regiment of Foot (Royal Bengal Fusiliers).

During 1869, there was a dreadful outbreak of cholera which became so bad it became an epidemic. The 104th were in their barracks at Peshawar, situated on the famous North West Frontier, where they had arrived on 12 December 1868.

Since August 1869, there had been outbreaks of cholera in the camp. When the situation did not improve, Colonel Webber Desborough Harris, by now the commanding officer of the 104th, decided that his men should leave their barracks and go and live in the countryside for a period of time, to try and reduce the chances of his men contracting the disease, and alleviate the impact on those already afflicted by it.

At 3am on 11 September 1869, the 104th broke camp, and made for the hills. After marching for many hours they made camp for the night, during which twenty-seven men died of cholera. The next night they made camp at the base of Cherat Hill, where they remained until 9 December 1869, when the doctor determined that all of their number were finally devoid of the disease.

With the end of epidemic the regiment returned to its barracks at Peshawar, arriving there on 12 December 1869. It was then that the regiment's officers presented Mrs Harris with her gold replica Victoria Cross, for her tireless efforts in looking after and caring for the officers and men of the regiment who had been stricken by cholera. The presentation of the gold medal was carried out by the Peshawar garrison's commanding officer, General Sir Samuel Browne, himself a holder of the Victoria Cross. The medal included an inscription which read;

> Replica of the Victoria Cross, in gold, presented to Mrs Webber Harris by the officers of the 104th Bengal Fusiliers, for her indomitable pluck, during the cholera epidemic of 1869. It was necessary to have Queen Victoria's special permission for this replica to be made.

There was no formal citation issued with the award as it was not an official award, and no report of its presentation was recorded in the *London Gazette*. The gold replica Victoria Cross is now part of Lord Ashcroft's collection.

The Second World War saw the Victoria Cross awarded on 182 occasions to just 181 people. To have even been considered for the award means that each person was undoubtedly an extremely brave individual, and those included within these pages are certainly no exception.

Chapter One

Charles Groves Wright Anderson

Charles Anderson was, without doubt, a remarkable man. Born on 12 February 1897, at Newlands in Cape Town, South Africa, during the First World War he served with the British army, reaching the rank of captain, and was awarded the Military Cross. In the Second World War he served in the 2nd/19th Australian Imperial Force, and was awarded the Victoria Cross for his gallantry. He survived the war and died on 11 November 1988 aged 91.

He was one of five children born to Alfred and Emma Anderson. When Charles was 3 years old, the family moved to what is today, Kenya, but in 1900 was known as the East Africa Protectorate. Their new home was a farm called Mount Margaret, on the outskirts of Nairobi. It would have been a great life for a young boy, most of his time spent outdoors, with a constant supply of hot sunny weather, an adventure that would usually only be found in the pages of a book.

In 1907, with his future education in mind, Charles, who by that time was 10, was sent back to England by his parents to live with an aunt and uncle, and when he turned 13, he enrolled as a pupil at St Brendan's College in Bristol. It wasn't unusual for boys of a certain class not to be living with their parents. Boarding school was the main cause for separation. It's just how life was back then, character building they called it. For a young man, or rather a boy, to have to stand on his own two feet and make his own decisions, was seen as part of his overall education.

Just three months after the outbreak of the First World War, he returned to his family in Africa, and in 1915, aged 18, he enlisted in the Calcutta Volunteer Battery. He was obviously an impatient, yet determined young man, as the following year showed. On 13 October 1916, he received a temporary commission as a lieutenant in the 2nd Battalion, 3rd Regiment, King's African Rifles. During his time serving with them, he was noted for his outstanding leadership qualities, especially whilst engaged in fighting the enemy. This particularly came to the fore during fighting at what was then called, Nhamacurra Portuguese East Africa, but which is today known as, Mozambique.

It was in July 1918 that he was awarded the Military Cross for his bravery, and was promoted to the rank of temporary captain, just prior to be being demobbed in February 1919. After the end of the war, he chose to return to Nairobi, where he became a gentleman farmer, having greatly enjoyed the previous occasions he had lived there.

In 1935, he emigrated to Australia with his wife, Edith, and their three children, with the family settling in a place called Fernhill at Crowther, in New South Wales. Although Edith was Australian, the couple had married in Nairobi on 21 February 1931, when Anderson was 33 years old.

With the Second World War looming, he was appointed as a captain in the 56th Battalion (Riverina Regiment) Militia, on 3 March 1939, and he was further promoted in October the same year, becoming a major.

These were troubled and difficult times for everybody, especially for couples with young children. Families would be split by the very nature of war, people understood that, but it was the uncertainty, the not knowing if they would ever see each other again, that was difficult to bear.

With the war just about to reach the end of its first year, and with Anderson still living in his adopted Australia, he volunteered for overseas service and transferred to the 2nd/19th Battalion, Australian Imperial Force on 1 July 1940, where he became the second in command.

In February 1941, after completing his basic training around Ingleburn and then Bathurst, he was deployed to Malaya, along with the 2nd/19th Battalion, Australian Imperial Force, which was part of the 22nd Brigade, of the 8th Division, primarily to bolster the garrison there, due to concerns about what Japan's military intentions were in the area. Because of his experience in jungle warfare he was placed in charge of training the battalion's soldiers in how to use the jungle as a 'friend' and after just six months in theatre he had become the battalion's commanding officer with a promotion to the rank of lieutenant colonel.

Anderson was deceptive to look at, as his physical appearance didn't paint a true picture of his full capabilities. He wasn't the tallest man in the world, nor the thickest set, plus he wore glasses, which didn't make him look the most obvious of natural leaders. But he was the classic example of 'don't judge a book by its cover'. He was everything that could be hoped for in a fighting man, and more.

Japan had entered the war with a massive declaration of what her intentions were in the Pacific. Firstly, her forces carried out a surprise attack at Pearl Harbor, which intentionally or not, brought America into the Second World War. Almost simultaneously, her forces also landed on the north-east coast of Malaya, in the Kota Bahru area and hurriedly sent troops along the western coast of the Malay Peninsula from Thailand.

Part of the problem had come about because the Allies had totally underestimated the Japanese: with the threat that they posed, their abilities and their culture. There was almost a conceit on the part of the British in what they thought of as their own superiority, against a lesser enemy who ultimately would cause them no real problem.

The British government had failed to make defensive improvements to the northern shores of Singapore, which were separated from Malaya by the Straits of Johore. What made that even more unbelievable was that it was Lieutenant Colonel Arthur Percival, General Officer Commanding Malaya Command – the man in charge of all British and Commonwealth troops in Malaya and Singapore – who had identified the potential weaknesses. The number of aircraft allocated to the Malaya peninsula was 84, despite the chiefs of staff having agreed that the required number of aircraft required for the Far East as a whole should be 336 front-line aircraft. At a conference held in Singapore in October 1940 the same chiefs of staff recommended that the figure of 336 should be raised to 582. By 7 December 1941, the number of serviceable aircraft in Malaya was only 134, but they did have 76,300 troops on the ground, although for some inexcusable reason, there were no Allied tank units in either Malaya or Singapore.

Initially Anderson's 2nd/19th Battalion were not committed to the fighting, but after the Japanese advance had pushed the British Commonwealth troops back to Johore by the middle of January 1942, the 2nd/19th Battalion was sent to the west coast of Malaya to support the hard-pressed Allied forces, who were trying their best to stem the tide of the Japanese advance. It meant there was now a mixed force of Australian and Indian troops doing their best to prevent being overrun by a determined enemy.

Unlike some of his fellow senior officers, Anderson was flexible and had the ability to change his tactics to whatever circumstances he found himself in at the time. He had the additional advantage that his men respected and believed in him, and when a commanding officer had that type of commitment from his men, he could achieve much more than many would have believed possible.

Anderson was a rare breed as a commanding officer in the field, because he was not only prepared to lead from the front, but also had the ability to be able to do so. Some officers were tactically brilliant on a map and getting others to put their plans into operation, but when men saw their commanding officer leading them, standing shoulder to shoulder with them as the bullets were whizzing past their heads, they gave so much more of themselves. Anderson was the type of commanding officer that most men would want in such a situation.

During their journey from Muar to Parit Sulong, whilst the Allies were in the process of collectively retreating to Yong Peng to join up with the main force heading for Singapore, the fighting was often of a very basic nature. It was ugly and unpleasant. Anderson found himself leading bayonet charges direct into Japanese forces, and becoming involved in brutal hand-to-hand fighting. These were not the normal actions of a senior officer of Anderson's rank.

The Battle of Muar took place between 18 and 22 January 1942, during which time Anderson was in command of a force of men who, although small in number, were extremely effective, managing to knock out ten Japanese tanks in the process.

Upon reaching the small town of Parit Sulong, Anderson and his men discovered their way was blocked because the main bridge was already in the hands of the Japanese, who in turn had set up defensive machine-gun positions around the bridge. The Australians were quickly surrounded and a heavy battle ensued for several days in the town. The Allied troops who were at Yong Peng under the command of Gordon Bennett, tried to break through the Japanese lines to reinforce Anderson's men, but were unable to do so, and without reinforcements, Anderson and his troops could not capture the bridge, despite trying numerous times to do so. Heavily outnumbered, Anderson's Australian and Indian troops were attacked and harassed continuously by Japanese tanks, machine-gun, mortar and air attacks and suffered heavy casualties. Against overwhelming odds they held their position for several days, fighting hard and refusing to surrender. During the battle, Anderson had tried to evacuate the wounded by using an ambulance, but the Japanese would not let the vehicles pass across the bridge.

Anderson and his men's position became more untenable as time went on, and they were eventually left with no option but to try and fight their way out of their position, and make it the 8 miles to Yong Peng. To achieve this was not straightforward, as it involved travelling through enemy-held territory, and as a unit they made too much noise and were too big a target. Anderson ordered his men to split up and escape through the jungle to Yong Peng, where the main Allied forces were situated waiting to make their way to Singapore. In essence, it was every man for himself. Although maybe somewhat unorthodox in its application, Anderson had calculated that greater numbers of his men would more likely escape if they split up rather than if they stayed together.

Malaya, which later became Malaysia, has an equatorial climate, which means it is hot all year round. The monsoon season usually lasts from November until March, so areas of the country can also be quite wet, but it can still be sunny and relatively cool. The sun would have been at its hottest between 11am and 3pm. Even in January the average daytime temperature can be in the early 30s and during the night as high as the early 20s. Added to that was the extra heat of humidity.

The weather conditions alone would have been difficult enough to contend with. Anderson and his men would have needed to be drinking a lot of water throughout the course of the day so as not to dehydrate. Add to these conditions having to fight a war in a jungle type of environment, and it really highlights the achievements of Anderson and his men. Fighting an unforgiving enemy in an extremely tough environment would have tested the strongest men both physically and mentally. Anderson and his men stood up to the challenge admirably.

Anderson had to make the difficult decision of leaving all his wounded men behind – some 150 men in total – such had been the intensity of the fighting. These men were left behind in the belief that the Japanese would take care of them, giving more of them chance to survive. Unfortunately, Anderson's interpretation of the words 'take care of' was obviously totally different to that of the Japanese Imperial Guards Division of the Imperial Japanese army.

It was later reported that the Japanese Imperial Guards kicked and beat some of the wounded Australian and Indian prisoners of war with their rifle butts until they were dead. Some of them were tied up with wire in the middle of the road and machine-gunned. As if that wasn't bad enough, the dead bodies were then doused in petrol by the Japanese, set on fire, and then repeatedly run over, by Japanese vehicles. According to some sources concerning the atrocity, there are anecdotal accounts by some local people that report Allied PoWs had their hands tied behind their backs with wire, each man was then tied to the man in front of him, and as a group they were forced to stand on the wall of a bridge. A Japanese soldier then shot the first man in the line, and as he fell his momentum pulled the next man, and so on, causing all of them to fall into the Simpang Kiri River and drown.

Lieutenant Ben Hackney of the 2nd/19th Battalion, Australian Imperial Force, feigned death and managed to escape into the jungle from the site of the massacre. Hackney was an incredible individual who must have had an extreme desire to live. He crawled through the undergrowth for six weeks, with little to eat or drink. Now some may think this was nothing particularly outstanding, but he did that with two broken legs. Many men would have not have been as resilient, and simply have given up. He was eventually recaptured, but thankfully for him, the Japanese soldiers who discovered him did not realise he had escaped from the massacre site at Parit Sulong. Hackney survived the war despite being held in a number of Japanese PoW camps for some three years, and being made to work as part of the labour force on the notorious Burma Railway. He and two other survivors gave evidence about the massacre to Allied war crimes investigators after the war.

The man who was ultimately held responsible for the massacre at Parit Sulong, was Lieutenant General Takuma Nishimura, who was the commanding officer of the Japanese Imperial Guards, and who was later one of those in charge of the Japanese occupying forces in Singapore

He was indirectly involved in the Sook Ching Massacre in Singapore, but 'retired' from the Japanese army in 1942 and made the military governor of Sumatra. After the war, he was tried by a British military court in Singapore in relation to the Sook Ching massacre, and rather than receive the death penalty as many had expected him to, Nishimura received a life sentence, of which he served just four years, before being sent back to Japan to complete his sentence. On his way back to Japan by ship, it stopped off at Hong Kong en route. Australian Military Police boarded the vessel and forcibly removed Nishimura, before then charging him in relation to the Parit Sulong massacre. Nishimura was taken to Manus Island in New Guinea, where he was placed before an Australian military court. Evidence was presented stating that Nishimura had been the person who ordered the shootings of the wounded Australian and Indian soldiers at Parit Sulong and the subsequent destruction of their bodies. He was found guilty and executed by hanging on 11 June 1951. At least those Australian and Indian troops who had been so brutally and cowardly murdered, whilst unable to defend themselves, had been avenged in some small way by Nishimura's execution

As for Charles Anderson, he was rightly awarded the Victoria Cross for both his leadership and brave actions in Muar and during the subsequent retreat to Parit Sulong. His VC citation, as listed in the *London Gazette* on Friday 13 February 1942, read as follows:

The King has been graciously pleased to approve the award of the Victoria Cross to:

Lieutenant Colonel Charles Groves Wright Anderson, MC. Australian Military Forces.

During the operations in Malaya from the 18th to 22nd January 1942, Lieutenant Colonel Anderson, in command of a small force, was sent to restore a vital position and to assist a Brigade. His Force destroyed ten enemy tanks. When later cut off, he defeated persistent attacks on his position from air and ground forces, and forced his way through the enemy lines to a depth of fifteen miles. He was again surrounded and subjected to very heavy and frequent attacks resulting in severe casualties to his force. He personally led an attack with great gallantry on the enemy who were holding a bridge, and succeeded in destroying four guns. Lieutenant Colonel Anderson throughout all this fighting, protected his wounded and refused to leave them.

He obtained news by wireless of the enemy position and attempted to fight his way back through eight miles of enemy occupied country. This proved to be impossible and the enemy were holding too strong a position for any attempt to be made to relieve him.

On the 19th January Lieutenant Colonel Anderson was ordered to destroy his equipment and make his way back as best he could round the enemy position.

Throughout the fighting, which lasted for four days, he set a magnificent example of brave leadership, determination and outstanding courage. He not only showed fighting qualities of a very high order, but throughout exposed himself to danger without any regard to his own personal safety.

After escaping from Parit Sulong, Anderson made his way to Singapore, as the remaining Allied forces withdrew across the Johore Straits causeway to set up their defence positions in preparation for the Japanese attack that they all knew was coming. Shortly after arriving in Singapore, he was admitted to hospital, which meant that he missed the majority of the fighting following the Japanese landings at Singapore on 8 February 1942. As the situation became desperate for the Allied defenders, Anderson discharged himself from his sick bed on 13 February, and returned to his very understrength 2nd/19th Battalion, by then down to just 180 men from its original strength of 900. He continued to lead his men, despite his ailments, until the surrender was announced on 15 February 1942, after Percival's capitulation to the Japanese.

Anderson was taken prisoner and spent the following three years as a prisoner of war. He was the chief staff officer under Brigadier Arthur Varley of the 22nd Brigade in 'A' Force, who were the first group of Allied PoWs to be held at Changi prison and who volunteered to move to a new location where they were told there would be abundant food and a healthy climate. In reality the group of 3,000 men were shipped to Burma and were used as slave labour to build what became known as the Burma Railway. Anderson survived the war and after his release from captivity he returned to Australia, where he returned to his family in New South Wales. He was demobbed from the army on 21 December 1945.

Anderson became a politician and threw himself into his new-found role with the same commitment and passion as he had done whilst a soldier. His political career saw him active between 1949 and 1961, during which time he held the seat for the Division of Hume in 1949, lost it in 1951 and regained it again in 1955, before losing it in 1961, which resulted in his retirement from politics. He died in Canberra in 1988, and his Victoria Cross is displayed at the Australian War Memorial at Canberra.

CHARLES GROVES WRIGHT ANDERSON

From everything that has been written about Anderson he appears to be one of the most unassuming and unlikeliest individuals to have ever been awarded the VC, but it is evidence of just how some otherwise ordinary men have the capacity to find an inner strength, steely determination and an ability to elevate themselves to be able to carry out super-human acts of bravery, and compassion for others, whilst putting their own lives at risk, when called upon to do so in a time of war.

Chapter Two

Premindra Singh Bhagat

Premindra Bhagat was born in Gorakhpur, United Provinces of Agra, on 13 October 1918. His father, Surendra Singh Bhagat, was an executive engineer working for the provincial government. His mother died in 1927 when he was just 9 years old. The loss of his mother at such a young age would have had quite an effect on him, especially as being able to show much in the way of emotion in a very male-dominated society, would not have met with too much in the way of compassion from other male family members.

When Premindra was still only 11 years old, he started attending the Royal Indian Military College in Dehradun, the interim capital of the state of Uttarakhand. Academically he was just like many of his peers, an average student. There were no obvious or immediate signs that he was destined for military greatness, but as would be proven in Premindra's case, just because a young man isn't an academic genius, does not for one second mean he does not possess humility, along with bravery and courage.

He left the Royal Indian Military College in 1937, and in June the same year entered the Indian Military Academy, also situated in Dehradun. By this time he was 19. Once again his instructors marked him as no more than an average student academically, but he was well thought of in a sporting sense, taking part in as many sports as he could at the college, where he was the captain of both the tennis and squash teams. Maybe it was the sudden death of his father in a riding accident in 1938 that made Premindra finally knuckle down to his military studies. But whatever the reason was, he did sufficiently well in his final year's exams to be commissioned on 15 July 1939 as a second lieutenant in the British Indian army. His commission saw him serving with the Royal Bombay Sappers and Miners, a regiment of the Corps of Engineers of the Indian army. Soon after the Second World War had broken out across Europe, he was posted to the 21st Field Company of Engineers, who were stationed at Pune in September 1939, which is the second biggest city in the Indian state of Maharashtra.

For the next year, Premindra and his men were involved in nothing more intense and dangerous than training exercises, but all that changed on 23 September 1940, when they were sent to East Africa as part of the 10th Indian Infantry Brigade, which in turn was part of the 5th Indian Infantry Division.

The man in charge of the 10th Indian Brigade was Brigadier William Slim, a proper old school fighting man who had served in the First World War and been wounded on two occasions, and on 7 February 1918 he was awarded the Military Cross, whilst serving as a second lieutenant with the West India Regiment in Mesopotamia during the latter months of 1916. He was wounded for a third time on 21 January 1941 whilst in command of the 10th Indian Brigade in Eritrea, when his position was strafed by aircraft during the brigade's advance on Agordat.

On 6 November 1940, Brigadier Slim launched an attack on the Fort of Gallabat, which is situated on the outskirts of the village of Gallabat, and is a border crossing point with neighbouring Ethiopia. The main reason for the assault was that up until July 1940, the Fort of Gallabat had been held by a small British garrison under the command Wilfred Thesiger, who was ousted by Italian forces who had advanced on the fort from what was Italian East Africa.

The initial assault plan by Brigadier Slim was a success, with elements of the 3rd Royal Garhwal Rifles leading the way. But the victory was short lived as enemy forces quickly counter-attacked, regained the fort and forced Lieutenant Colonel Taylor's Garhwal Rifles to withdraw.

To ensure their retreat went unhindered and they were not followed, Taylor had ordered his sappers to obstruct the Italians. Part of what they did was to fill up two broken down and beyond repair tanks with explosives and place them under a culvert, but only one of the tanks exploded, and the blast wasn't powerful enough to bring down the culvert. This wasn't good news for Taylor's men. Without any thought or consideration for his own safety, Second Lieutenant Premindra Singh Bhagat suddenly ran out from behind his cover and made his way to the culvert. In doing so he quickly brought himself to the attention of the Italian forces who were in pursuit. Before he had made it across the open ground, the Italians opened fire, sending a cascade of bullets heading in his direction. Fortunately for Bhagat, none of the bullets found him as their target. He made it to the culvert and the unexploded tank, reset the detonator and made his way safely back to cover without any of the Italians quick or accurate enough to hit him. Shortly afterwards the second tank exploded and the culvert collapsed, allowing the Indian troops to make good their escape.

Not surprisingly Bhagat was recommended for the Military Cross for his heroism and bravery that day. But maybe what is surprising, was that the recommendation for his well-deserved award, was not approved, the reason why isn't clear, instead he received a mention in despatches.

On 31 January 1941, Second Lieutenant Bhagat was sent on a reconnaissance mission towards the Ethiopian town of Metemma, on the border with Sudan. He was in charge of a mobile column, which consisted of the 3rd/12th Royal Frontier Force Rifles and a detachment of the 21st Field Company. En route, Bhagat's Bren gun carrier, a small type of personnel carrier, drove through a heavily mined stretch of road, and in doing so ran over and set off two of the mines. The second of these damaged the carrier beyond repair and killed two of those on board, including the driver. Bhagat continued the journey on board another Bren gun carrier.

The Commonwealth War Graves Commission website records the names of four Indian soldiers who died on 31 January 1941, all of whom are commemorated on the Khartoum Memorial in Sudan. Two of these men served with the 3rd Battalion, 14th Punjab Regiment, another with the 6th Rajputana Rifles, and one with King George V's Own Bengal Sappers and Miners.

As the column carefully and slowly meandered its way up the road, Second Lieutenant Bhagat continually alighted from his vehicle to defuse land mines by hand. But this wasn't just on a few occasions, this devotion to duty continued through some 15 minefields, which took four days to safely negotiate, a distance of 55 miles, without food or rest.

His selfless actions over that four-day period undoubtedly saved many lives, while he bravely and courageously unpicked each of the mines one at a time, not knowing if the next one was the one that was booby-trapped, and would be the one that would blow him to pieces. To be able to continually remain so calm for such a protracted period of time under that much pressure, knowing that if he made just one mistake it would not only cost him his life but the resultant explosion might also injure and kill many of his men, was an amazing feat by any standard. For many miles of this uncertain journey, he also had the added complication of being under enemy fire.

Two days into this marathon, the Bren gun carrier he was travelling in ran over and detonated a mine, this resulted in one of his ear drums being perforated. He was evacuated to the safety of a British military hospital in Khartoum, which was run by the Royal Army Medical Corps.

Once again he did not receive the Military Cross. On this occasion there was no being mentioned in despatches. This time it was the big one. He was awarded the Victoria Cross later that same month. Four months later he was presented with the ribbon by General Archibald Percival Wavell, in June 1941 at Asmara, the capital of Eritrea. Wavell was the commander in chief, India between July 1941 and June 1943, and a distinguished army officer who served for a total of forty-two years in the British army, between 1901 and 1943, which saw him serve in the second Boer War, the First World War, as well as the Second World War.

Bhagat's formal investiture service where he received his Victoria Cross took place at the viceroy's House in Delhi on 10 November 1941. His award was handed to him by Lord Linlithgow, Viceroy of India. A very well-deserved award for an extremely brave young man.

He would have been rightfully extremely proud of his achievement, despite the fact that he hadn't been expected to achieve that much at military college by his instructors; he proved that he was made of much stronger stuff then he had ever been given credit for.

In essence, the award of his Victoria Cross was the end of Bhagat's fighting war, although he would remain in the Indian army until 1974. Initially, his new-found status as an Indian who had been awarded the highest possible medal for gallantry for a member of British or Commonwealth forces, in the shape of the Victoria Cross, was used to good effect when he became a recruiting officer for the Bombay Sappers, and a very successful one at that.

Three months after receiving his Victoria Cross, he married Mohini Bhandari, who at 19 years old was four years younger than he was. Her father was a colonel in the Indian Army Medical Corps, who no doubt would have been extremely proud that his beloved daughter had not only married an army officer, but one who was deemed to have been brave and worthy enough to have been awarded the Victoria Cross.

After his successful stint as a recruiting officer, he was made the commanding officer of No. 484 Field Company, who having been schooled in jungle warfare during 1943, ended up fighting the Japanese in the jungles of Burma.

In January 1945, he was sent to England to attend a course at the Camberley Staff College, and became one of the first Indian officers to do so. He returned to India at the end of the war in August 1945. But in June 1946, less than a year later, he returned to England to attend an engineering course, before being promoted to the rank of captain on 1 July 1946.

Returning to India in 1947 he was further promoted to the rank of major and sent to serve with the Punjab Boundary Force, whose main task was to maintain law and order in the region, in the immediate aftermath of Indian Independence, which on 15 August 1947 partitioned British India into the two new countries of India and Pakistan. This also meant the partition of the provinces of Bengal and Punjab between the two new countries. With the dissolution of the Punjab Boundary Force on 1 September 1947, Bhagat was promoted to the rank of acting lieutenant colonel and put in charge of the Royal Engineers of the 4th Infantry Division.

Over the following twelve years, Bhagat was further promoted and found himself in charge of both training and different military units.

On 29 August 1959, he was placed in command of Indian Military Intelligence at army headquarters. Part of his time in this role was spent undertaking a detailed and in-depth assessment of the potential danger India was in militarily, from the possibility of an attack from China. For some reason his comprehensive report was ignored, and on 20 October 1962 Chinese troops advanced into Ladakh, a region in the Indian state of Jammu and Kashmir. They also crossed over the McMahon Line, which was the border between the Tibetan region of China and the North East region of India.

The war lasted for one month and one day, and ended when China declared a ceasefire and withdrew its troops to the pre-war borders. Despite this it was a resounding victory for the Chinese, who were simply intent on flexing their military muscles against what they had seen as Indian belligerence, in relation to a series of border clashes between the two nations. These included India's decision to grant political asylum to the Dalai Lama, and India's 'Forward Policy', which had seen her place military outposts along the border between the two countries. Some of these border posts had actually been set up on the Chinese side of the border. The war was also notable because neither side deployed either their navy or airforce into the battle, and it was fought at altitudes of 14,000ft.

Bhagat remained in the army until 1974, it might have even been longer, but his retirement came not too long after he was overlooked for the position of chief of the army staff.

That steely determination and desire to do his duty to the best of his ability, with others in mind, which resulted in the young officer being awarded the Victoria Cross, were the same when he was still serving his country as a soldier thirty years later.

The citation for his award of the Victoria Cross was announced by the War office, and appeared in the *London Gazette* on 10 June 1941, and read as follows:

> His Majesty the King has been graciously pleased to approve of the award of the Victoria Cross to the undermentioned officer:
>
> Second Lieutenant Premindra Singh Bhagat, Corps of Indian Engineers (serving with Royal Bombay Sappers and Miners).
>
> For most conspicuous gallantry on active service in the Middle East. During the pursuit of the enemy following the capture of Metemma on the night of 31 January-1 February 1941, Second Lieutenant Bhagat was in command of a section of a Field Company, sappers and miners, detailed to accompany the leading mobile troops (Bren carriers) to clear the road and adjacent areas of mines. For a period of four days and over a distance of 55 miles this officer in the leading carrier led the column. During this period, he himself detected and personally supervised the clearing of no less than 15 minefields of varying dimensions. Speed being essential, he worked at high pressure from dawn to dusk each day. On two occasions when his carrier was blown up with casualties to others, and on a third occasion when ambushed and under close enemy fire, he himself carried straight on with his task. He refused relief when worn out with strain and fatigue and with one eardrum punctured by an explosion, on the grounds that he was now better qualified to continue his task to the end.
>
> His coolness, persistence over a period of 96 hours, and gallantry, not only in battle, but throughout the long period when the safety of the Column and the speed at which it could advance were dependent on his personal efforts, were of the highest order.

Chapter Three

Edward Colquhoun Charlton

The award of the Victoria Cross to Edward Colquhoun Charlton was well deserved. It shows a driven and determined individual prepared and willing to carry out an act of daring and out and out bravery, for the benefit of others, knowing that in doing so he was putting his own life at risk.

It is also worth noting that the award to Edward Charlton was one of two Victoria Crosses awarded to men who died on 21 April 1945, whilst fighting in Germany. The other being Ian Oswald Liddell, whose award related to an incident that took place on 3 April 1945, he was then subsequently killed in action 21 April 1945, when a single bullet killed a colleague of his, penetrating his head, before striking him and killing him as well.

The other point worth noting is that the Victoria Cross in question, was the last one that was physically awarded during the course of the Second World War, when it was presented to the parents of Edward Charlton by King George VI at Buckingham Palace on 2 May 1946.

Edward Colquhoun Charlton, VC, was born on 15 June 1920 in County Durham. When the war began, he had just had his nineteenth birthday. He enlisted as a guardsman in the 2nd Battalion, Irish Guards, of the Guards Armoured Division in the British army, and served with them as they fought their way across Europe during the Second World War. Whilst serving with them he carried out an action on 21 April 1945, which saw him awarded the Victoria Cross.

Guardsman Charlton was the co-driver of a tank that was supporting an infantry platoon. They occupied the village of Wistedt, in Germany, which the German army then attempted to re-take. The German forces outnumbered those of the British, and consisted mainly of officer cadets under the command of experienced instructor officers, all of whom were supported by three self-propelled guns. During the action, three of the four Irish Guards tanks were badly damaged, while Charlton's had been disabled by a complete electrical failure before the attack had even begun. Rather than play no active part in the action, Charlton decided to dismount the Browning machine gun from the tank's turret and support the infantry.

It soon became apparent that the defensive positions of the Irish Guards were in danger of being overrun by the German attackers. Charlton, realising the precarious situation they were in, and using his own initiative, took the machine gun and advanced in full view of the attacking Germans, firing the weapon from his hip, and inflicting heavy casualties upon them as he went, not giving the German attackers any respite in which to reorganise and retire. He continued his bold attack, even when he sustained a wound to his left arm. To ease his situation but to maintain the effectiveness of his attack, Charlton placed the machine gun on a fence to enable him to maintain his rate and intensity of fire and keep the Germans at bay. He launched a further attack on the enemy forces before he was once again hit by more enemy fire, shattering one of the bones in his left arm and making it totally useless. Now with only one good arm, Charlton carried on his attack until he suffered a further wound. This, and the resultant loss of blood, caused the guardsman to collapse. His courageous and selfless disregard for his own safety allowed the rest of the Irish Guards' troop and infantry to escape. Having finally been put out of action by the Germans, he was captured, taken prisoner, but later died from his serious wounds whilst in the hospital wing of the prisoner of war camp at Bremervorde in Germany. He was initially buried at the Elsdorf cemetery. In January 1947, he was re-interred by the German authorities in Wistedt Cemetery, in Rhade, before just one month later being exhumed by the Allies and buried in the Becklingen War Cemetery, at Soltau, Germany, which is about 30 miles south of Hamburg.

Charlton was awarded the Victoria Cross posthumously, it was the last one awarded from an action in the European theatre of war, and the last one ever awarded to a member of the Irish Guards. Unusually, much of the citation was based on German accounts of what took place as most of Charlton's later actions were not witnessed by any of the officers or men of the British infantry or Irish Guards who were present.

Edward Charlton's mother subsequently decided to donate all her son's wartime medals, including his Victoria Cross, to the Irish Guards Regimental Headquarters, which are now displayed at The Guards Museum, Wellington Barracks, London.

The citation for the award of Edward Charlton's VC, which appeared in the *London Gazette* dated Thursday 2 May 1946, reads as follows:

The King has been graciously pleased to approve the posthumous award of the Victoria Cross to:

No.2722614 Guardsman Edward Colquhoun Charlton, Irish Guards.

In Germany on the morning of 21st April 1945, Guardsman Charlton was co-driver in one tank of a troop which, with a platoon of infantry, seized the village of Wistedt. Shortly afterwards the enemy attacked this position under cover of an artillery concentration and in great strength, comprising, as it later transpired, a battalion of the 15 Panzer Grenadiers supported by six self-propelled guns. All the tanks, including Guardsman Charlton's were hit; the infantry were hard pressed and in danger of being overrun.

Whereupon, entirely on his own initiative, Guardsman Charlton decided to counter attack the enemy. Quickly recovering the Browning from his damaged tank, he advanced up the road in full view of the enemy, firing the Browning from his hip. Such was the boldness of his attack and the intensity of his fire that he halted the leading enemy company, inflicting heavy casualties on them. This effort at the same time bought much needed relief to our own infantry.

For ten minutes Guardsman Charlton fired in this manner, until wounded in the left arm. Immediately, despite intense enemy fire, he mounted his machine gun on a nearby fence, which he used to support his wounded left arm. He stood firing thus for a further ten minutes until he was again hit in the left arm which fell away shattered and useless.

Although twice wounded and suffering from loss of blood. Guardsman Charlton again lifted his machine gun on to the fence, now having only one arm with which to fire and reload. Nevertheless, he still continued to inflict casualties on the enemy, until finally, he was hit for a third time and collapsed. He died later of his wounds in enemy hands. The heroism and determination of this Guardsman in his self-imposed task were beyond all praise. Even his German captors were amazed at his valour.

Guardsman Charlton's courageous and self-sacrificing action not only inflicted extremely heavy casualties on the enemy and retrieved his comrades from a desperate situation, but also enabled the position to be speedily recaptured.

At the time of his death, Charlton was just 24 years old. He was buried at the Becklingen War Cemetery, in the Niedersachsen region of Germany. There is a plaque with his name on it in St John's Church, Old Trafford, Manchester. Another plaque can be found in Old Trafford Boys' School, Manchester, and the Manchester Abattoir Memorial, Phillips Park Cemetery, Manchester.

The award of the Victoria Cross to Guardsman Charlton, for his bravery at Wistedt in Germany, just eighteen days before the end of the fighting, was the 177th and final one presented for bravery during the Second World War. It was also the sixtieth one awarded to a soldier from the British army.

Edward's father, Albert Charlton, had served during the First World War. Before the war he had been an apprentice butcher, so when he enlisted in the army, instead of being sent to serve in an Infantry regiment on the Western Front, he was posted to the Army Service Corps and sent out to what was then German East Africa, but which today is known as Tanzania. His job there was to purchase and slaughter cattle to feed the British military personnel who were serving in the region.

Edward's elder brother, John, also saw service during the Second World War, with the RAF.

An interesting article about Edward and his family appeared on a BBC website under the heading, *WW2 People's War – An Archive of World War Two Memories*. The article was written by Edward's younger brother, Alwyn, and concerns a family holiday to Belgium that took place just before the beginning of the Second World War.

At the bottom of the article it was pointed out that the copyright remained with the author. As it was written in 2005, Alwyn would have been 77 years old at the time and, if still alive today (2019), he would be 91. Unfortunately, the closest, contactable, living relative was a fifth cousin, twice removed, who sadly had no contact with the immediate family.

The article talks about Edward at the very beginning of the war and is all the more poignant as it was written by his brother, albeit in his twilight years. With that in mind, it has been included here, but from a third person perspective.

The article begins with Alwyn talking about what many might think today was a very unusual choice of holiday destination for the time, especially taking into account how volatile Europe had become with the smouldering volcano of Germany's Nazi Party.

It was August 1939, just a matter of days before the hostilities of the Second World War began in earnest, when Alwyn, Edward and their parents arrived in Ostend, Belgium at the start of their holiday, possibly with great anticipation about what new experiences were going to unfold for them all.

Alwyn recalls that on 31 August 1939 they paid a visit to Dunkirk, and were all suitably impressed with the long stretches of beach, before returning to Ostend later that day. It was still light when they arrived, and the first thing that drew their attention to the unfolding events, was when they noticed a large number of Belgium soldiers milling about, specifically on the street corners, where they went about stopping anyone and everyone who was riding a bicycle, and commandeered their cycles.

Alwyn's father, Albert, made some enquiries to try and discover what all the commotion was about. The answer – because the outbreak of war was imminent – was a shock to them all. All of a sudden things became very real. Alwyn's father had learnt that the next boat leaving Ostend for England, wasn't until 9am the following morning, but after that, nothing could be guaranteed, so he purchased tickets for the four of them, and returned to the hotel where they were staying, and, along with their mother, calmly began packing their bags. There was no panic, or none that Alwyn and Edward's parents displayed, but despite this resilience, it must have been a worrying time for the parents, whereas maybe for Edward and Alwyn, it was more of an exciting adventure than anything else.

They caught the 9am boat as planned, and made their way across the English Channel, in what Alwyn remembers as being a relatively packed boat, which he later understood was a last chance of escape. The boat arrived safely at Folkestone some hours later, the journey being without any dramas.

As their holiday in Belgium had been cut short, they went to visit an uncle who lived somewhere in Kent, in a town that Alwyn couldn't remember the name of. They stayed there for the rest of the day and overnight, before making their way back home to Manchester, where they arrived later that same day, after catching a train from London, which he recalls was a Saturday.

The following morning Alwyn remembers, he, his parents and Edward sat around the radio set and listened whilst Prime Minister, Neville Chamberlain, announced that Britain had declared war on Germany. Things started happening very quickly after that. The next day being Monday, 4 September 1939, Alwyn found out that all the children who attended his school were being evacuated, and that he was being sent to live in Macclesfield in Cheshire, which was his first experience of being separated from his parents and brother Edward.

After saying goodbye to his family, he caught a train along with his school friends, to Macclesfield. On his arrival he found himself billeted with a family who had two sons, and lived in a nice house in a pleasant part of town, close to a very big country house, which fortunately for Alwyn was to be his new school, although some lessons, such as science, took place at the local county school where they had science laboratories.

The family he was living with were nice people as he recalled, he got on well with his foster parents as well as their two sons, but that changed somewhat when their elder son received his call-up papers. They resented that Alwyn's brother, John, who was already serving in the army had been posted to serve in Palestine, which they thought was a safe posting, but despite not really knowing which regiment their own son would be allocated to or where he might be sent to, they got it into their heads that it would be somewhere that would mean fighting against the Germans. Ironically, had he been posted to Palestine, he would have been in just as much danger. It was not the safe haven they thought it to be.

The following year Alwyn's uncle's house in Kent was bombed by the Luftwaffe, so he and his family travelled to Manchester and moved in with Alwyn's parents for the duration of the war. By the spring of 1940, Alwyn's school had reopened in Manchester, so he was able to bid farewell to his foster family and move back home with his parents. Despite living up north, the effects of the war were still felt. After the evacuation of over 300,000 British, French and Belgium troops from the beaches of Dunkirk in May 1940, some of those who had been rescued had been billeted in Alwyn's former primary school. To help out, his parents were asked if they could provide some home comforts for a small group of the soldiers, a request which they agreed to. For a period of time two of the soldiers spent some evenings sleeping in the Charltons' home until proper accommodation could be found for them.

The summer of 1940 was a relatively quiet period for Alwyn and his family, although at the end of it in September, Edward, who had celebrated his twentieth birthday in June, received his call-up papers, and was posted to the Irish Guards.

During the early winter months of 1940 there were many German air raids over Manchester, especially the Trafford Park area, which became a prime target. As Alwyn and his family lived close to it, they were always in a certain amount of danger. That was highlighted when one evening a large German bomb landed in the next door neighbours' back garden, but failed to detonate. If it had exploded, Alwyn and his parents would have undoubtedly been killed.

In the two worst December 1940 raids, which took place on the nights of 22/23 and 23/24 December 1940, 684 civilians were killed and more than 2,000 injured. Over the two nights, the German Luftwaffe dropped a total of 467 tons of high explosive bombs, along with some 2,000 incendiary devices.

In the summer of 1941, Alwyn and his parents received a nice surprise when there was a knock at the front door. It was the eldest of the three brothers, John. Because of security reasons he had not been allowed to inform his family that he was going to be back in England. Alwyn's father contacted Edward at his barracks and he was granted compassionate leave, which meant that for the first time in nearly five years, the entire family was back together, and although it was only for a short period of time, it was enjoyed by all the family, especially as the uncertainty of what lay ahead was never far from any of their thoughts.

With the brief family reunion over, both Edward and John had to return to their units. For John, this meant being posted to Canada where he retrained to become a pilot with the RAF. After having qualified as a pilot and having returned from Canada, he became a night-time fighter pilot, before becoming an instructor, a role in which he continued until the end of the war. During the same period of time, Edward's battalion had changed to become part of the Guards Armoured Division, and he also retrained and became a tank driver.

After the D-Day landings in Normandy in June 1944, the war became more distant as the Luftwaffe became less effective. But Alwyn kept in regular contact with both John and Edward by way of letter. Alwyn recalled Edward's letters being particularly upbeat and full of the pride he had for his unit and the men with whom he worked.

Alwyn remembered a particularly spooky event that occurred in April 1945 involving his mother. One night she was asleep in bed with his father, when she suddenly sat bolt upright in their bed and started screaming and shouting about his brother Edward, 'It's Ed he's hurt, he's hurt, he's hurt.' His father eventually managed to calm her down, and she eventually went back to sleep.

Just three weeks later and the war had finally come to an end after six long years. His father received a letter in the post from the War Office to inform him and his wife that Edward was missing in action, known to be wounded, and believed to be a prisoner of war. Just a few weeks later another letter from the War Office arrived, this one informing Alwyn's parents, that Edward had now been classified as having been killed in action as his grave had been located. This they found particularly hard to take as by the time they had been informed of Edward's death, the war had been over for three weeks.

A year after Edward's death, his parents received another letter from the War Office, to inform them that he had been awarded the Victoria Cross for the acts of bravery which had sadly resulted in his subsequent death. The date and times mentioned in the letter coincided with the premonition Alwyn's mother had had when she had woken up screaming Edward's name.

If things had turned out slightly differently back in August 1939, when Edward Charlton was on holiday with his family in Belgium, and he and his family had missed that last boat, the men whose lives he saved by his actions when he was awarded his Victoria Cross, may never have made it through the final weeks of the war.

What is amazing about Edward Charlton, is the enormous level of courage and bravery he displayed, but more than that, it was the fact that a young man, who prior to the war had just been a normal member of the public, minding his own business and getting on with his life, just like everyone else, became a heroic individual after being called up to serve in the war.

Chapter Four

Leonard Cheshire

Leonard Cheshire was an unusual and remarkable individual. In keeping with that premise, so was the award of his Victoria Cross, which is usually awarded to an individual for a singular or an immediate sequence of acts of bravery. In Cheshire's case, it was for his actions over the course of his wartime operational service up to that point in time.

The citation for the award of his Victoria Cross included the following:

> This officer began his operational career in June 1940. Against strongly defended targets he soon displayed the courage and determination of an exceptional leader. He was always ready to accept extra risks to ensure success. Defying the formidable Ruhr defences, he frequently released his bombs from below 2,000 feet. Over Cologne in November 1940, a shell burst inside his aircraft, blowing out one side and starting a fire. Undeterred he went on to bomb his target. About this time he carried out a number of convoy patrols, in addition to his bombing missions. At the end of his first tour of operational duty in January 1941 he immediately volunteered for a second tour. Again he pressed home his attacks with the utmost gallantry. Berlin, Bremen, Cologne, Duisburg, Essen and Kiel were among the heavily defended targets which he attacked. When he was posted for instructional duties in January 1942, he undertook four more operational missions. He started a third operational tour in August 1942, when he was given command of a squadron. He led the squadron with outstanding skill on a number of missions before being appointed in March 1943 as a station commander. In October 1943 he undertook a fourth operational tour, relinquishing

the rank of group captain at his own request so that he could again take part in operations. He immediately set to work as the pioneer of a new method of marking enemy targets involving very low flying. In June 1944, when marking a target in a harbour at Le Havre in broad daylight and without cloud cover, he dived well below the range of the light batteries before releasing his marker bombs, and he came very near to being destroyed by the strong barrage which concentrated on him. During his fourth tour which ended in July 1944, Wing Commander Cheshire led his squadron personally on every occasion, always undertaking the most dangerous and difficult task of marking the target alone from a low level in the face of strong defences.

Wing Commander Cheshire's cold and calculated acceptance of risks is exemplified by his conduct in an attack on Munich in April 1944. This was an experimental attack to test out the new method of target marking at low level against a heavily defended target situated deep in Reich territory. Munich was selected at Wing Commander Cheshire's request because of the formidable nature of its light anti-aircraft and searchlight defences. He was obliged to follow in bad weather, a direct route which took him over the defences of Augsburg and thereafter he was continuously under fire. As he reached the target, flares were being released by our high flying aircraft. He was illuminated from above and below. All guns within range opened fire on him. Diving to 700 feet, he dropped his markers with great precision and began to climb away. So blinding were the searchlights that he almost lost control. He then flew over the city at 1,000 feet to assess the accuracy of his work and direct other aircraft. His own was badly hit by shell fragments, but he continued to fly over the target area until he was satisfied that he had done all in his power to ensure success. Eventually when he set course for base the task of disengaging himself from the defences proved even more hazardous than the approach. For a full twelve minutes after leaving the target area he was under withering fire, but he came safely through. Wing Commander Cheshire has now completed a total of 100 missions. In four years of fighting against 'the bitterest opposition' he has maintained a record of outstanding personal achievement, placing himself invariably in the forefront of the battle. What he did in the Munich operation was typical of the careful planning, brilliant execution and contempt for danger which has established for Wing Commander Cheshire a reputation second to none in Bomber Command.

This chapter has been written in a prequel type manner, so that the last has come first.

Geoffrey Leonard Cheshire, Baron Cheshire, VC, OM, DSO & Two Bars, DFC, was a group captain, the youngest one on the RAF, and one of the most highly decorated pilots of the Second World War. He was born at Chester in Cheshire, on 7 September 1917, and went on to study jurisprudence, at Merton College, Oxford. Whilst a student he was required to enlist in one of the university's service clubs, and he eventually ended up in the Oxford University Air Squadron. After successfully passing his course of basic piloting skills, he was commissioned as a pilot officer on 16 November 1937, and became part of the RAF Volunteer Reserve.

With the outbreak of the war, he was given a permanent commission in the RAF, assigned to Bomber Command and sent for training at RAF Hullavington and RAF Abingdon.

Cheshire was promoted to flying officer and was posted to RAF Driffield, where he was attached to 102 Squadron which flew Armstrong Whitworth Whitley twin-engine bomber aircraft. As a new pilot he was placed in the care of one of the squadron's more experienced pilots, Hugh 'Lofty' Long. He taught Cheshire a great deal about being a pilot. Long was both encouraging and demanding in equal amounts, but he undoubtedly went a long way in helping to make Cheshire the pilot he eventually became. Long emphasised to Cheshire that being a good pilot wasn't just about flying, it was knowing everything there was to know about the aircraft he was in control of, that way, nothing would ever become a surprise. He pushed Cheshire so that flying the aircraft become second nature, that way if a problem arose during the flight he could give it his fullest attention because he wouldn't have to think about the flying aspect of being a pilot.

One of the drills Long taught Cheshire was to seat him in the pilot's seat blindfolded and go through all the different aircraft drills. He also made him sit in the navigator's, wireless operator's, and the rear gunner's seats, so that he could get a feel for what each of them were going through during a mission.

Long emphasised to him that the aircraft wasn't just about the pilot who flew it, but the entire crew, and if that anyone of them wasn't on their game, that affected the entire team. He urged him to really get to know all those who were part of his crew, whether that was the flight crew or those who were part of the ground crew, and that meant understanding each of their concerns and the individual problems each of them was going through, whether it was work or home related.

On the night of 12/13 November 1940, Cheshire was sent on a mission to bomb a target near Cologne, but en route he discovered that reaching his intended target would not be possible because of heavy cloud and general bad weather. But rather than go all that way and not hit a target, he decided to attack Cologne's railway yards. He began his bombing run onto his target as the German defensive ground batteries opened up. Before he knew what was happening, Long's advice became a reality. Two anti-aircraft shells exploded so close to Cheshire's aircraft that it blew a large section out of the fuselage on the port side, and set off one of the aircraft's flares. Remembering what he had been taught by Long, there was no panic despite his aircraft being in a steep dive to which seemed there could only be one outcome. The fire was extinguished by the crew, Cheshire regained full control of the aircraft and managed to drop his bombs despite some heavy flak, and then make his way safely back to his base at Linton-on-Ouse.

For carrying out the attack in such a badly damaged aircraft, Cheshire was awarded the Distinguished Service Order. Sadly for Cheshire, Long was killed during a bombing mission over German-occupied Europe on 13 March 1941. His death hit Cheshire extremely hard, although he never let anybody know how he felt at the time.

In January 1941 he was posted to No. 35 Squadron where he flew the four-engine Handley Page Halifax bomber, and just two months later he was awarded the Distinguished Flying Cross, and the following month he was promoted to the rank of flight lieutenant.

When Arthur Harris took over Bomber Command in February 1942, he wanted to enhance the role of what his aircraft could do. He came up with the plan to conduct 1,000 aircraft bombing raids on Nazi targets in Germany. One such raid was carried out over Berlin on the night of 8/9 August 1942. This was a raid that Cheshire was involved in, as was his younger brother Christopher, who was flying a Halifax bomber for No. 76 Squadron. He did not return from the raid, having been shot down over Berlin.

In March 1943, and having completed his third tour of flying, Cheshire was officially no longer eligible for any further flying operations. He also found himself promoted to acting group captain and sent to RAF Marston Moor, at the rather tender of age of just 25. It was a role and a rank that he really didn't care for, as all he wanted to do was fly operationally, and at the rank of group captain that wasn't going to happen.

In September 1943, Cheshire had found an escape route and it came in the form of Commander Ralph Cochrane who was in charge of No. 5 Group, which included the famous No. 617 Squadron. But to get the transfer it meant Cheshire having to relinquish his rank of group captain, and step down to wing commander. As he would have done anything to get back to operational flying it was a move he made willingly.

The move suited both parties. It was most certainly what Cheshire was looking for, and Cochrane had been tasked with the destruction of the German V3 Long Range Gun facility which was situated in underground bunkers near Mimoyecques in the Pas de Calais region of France, and Cheshire was just the standard of pilot that Cochrane was looking for.

These guns, if allowed to go unchecked, could fire 500lb shells into the centre of London every minute, and as the guns were protected by 50ft of reinforced concrete, even blanket-bombing the area would have little if no effect. What was called for was pinpoint accurate bombing of the facility. The government turned to Barnes Wallis, the British inventor and scientist, to see if could help them with their operation. After working out all the relevant equations he was able to say that a 12,000lb bomb dropped from 20,000ft, could penetrate the German V3 facility, but it would have to be extremely accurate, so accurate that it would have to land within just 12 metres from the target. Bombing with that degree of accuracy was unheard of during the Second World War. Wallis had given the bomb the nickname 'Tallboy'.

After a couple of 'trial runs' that proved such a plan could work if executed extremely accurately, Arthur Harris called for a meeting on the subject to take place at High Wycombe in February 1944, to discuss the destruction of V3 site. At the meeting were Air Officer Commanding Bomber Command, Arthur Harris, Air Officer Commanding of the Pathfinder Force, Air Vice Marshal Bennett, and the Air Officer Commanding 5 Group Cochrane, who brought Cheshire along with him, and the meeting was chaired by the Deputy Air Officer Commander-in-Chief Robert Saundby. When Bennett was told the accuracy needed for the bombing raid, he dismissed the idea out of hand. Cheshire challenged this, claiming it could be done with a low level marker aircraft, but Bennett rejected this idea as well. The outcome of the meeting was that the idea was left with 5 Group to see if they could work out a solution, which pleased them no end, especially as the idea for Wallis's bomb needed more time before it was fully developed and ready to be operationally deployed.

In this equation the marker was everything, because if it didn't land on the mission's intended target then all attempts at successfully bombing that intended target would be totally ineffective: because a marker landing say 150 yards away would result in the bombers aiming for that instead of what they had set out to destroy.

On previous missions, Pathfinder squadrons had used the technique of dropping a group of markers on their intended target, but usually they would be attacking a factory complex or a harbour area, or a railway yard, where the group of markers was extremely effective. But a target that was hidden in an underground complex required an exactness about it, so the margin for error was minimal.

It was Cheshire who came up with the idea of dropping a singular marker, but being able to drop an accurate marker meant sacrificing the safety factor of height. Cochrane, who was in charge of the Pathfinder squadron, had as his main consideration, crew safety, and so not surprisingly deemed that markers could not be released at a height of 5,000ft to try and reduce the size of target for German defensive anti-aircraft batteries.

Despite this directive from Cochrane, Cheshire for one didn't stick to what he had been ordered to do. He and one of his colleagues, Australian Mick Martin, had worked out that dropping a marker from 5,000ft meant that the closest it would land to the intended target would be between 150 and 300 yards away, which was no good for what they needed to do. If the marker was so far off its target it would be a waste of time even thinking about bombing it, especially as there was every likelihood that not all the aircraft would return.

Martin had tried a sort of dive-bombing technique, which was not without its dangers. His dive began at 5,000ft at a 30 degree angle, all the way down to just 100ft, where he could accurately drop the marker, before quickly pulling the Lancaster bomber out of its dive, even though he knew full well that a Lancaster maybe wasn't the best aircraft in the world to try such a manoeuvre in. But it worked and was absolutely accurate, which was ultimately what they needed to be able to guarantee the destruction of the V3 facility.

Cheshire and Martin had now come up with an accurate method of achieving the squadron's goal, it just happened to be 4,900ft lower than Cochrane had given permission for. All they had to do was to convince him that it was right to let them put their plan into action. The discussion between the three men was had, and Cochrane gave it his approval, but with the caveat that he wanted to see that it worked for real, before they tried it for real on the V3 site at Mimoyecques. They decided on an aero engine factory at Limoges in France. Before this mission could go ahead, approval had to be given by the War Cabinet, because the factory was surrounded by houses, many of which were the homes of French people who worked at the factory. The other, and bigger, problem was that the factory was open 24 hours a day which meant there would always be French workers in the factory. It certainly wasn't going to be a good target on which to practise their marker system if it was going to result in the deaths of hundreds of innocent French civilians.

After due consideration and discussion, the mission was given the go ahead by the War Cabinet, but they added a caveat that no French civilians were to be killed, a tall order in the circumstances. The attack went ahead on the night of 8/9 February 1944. Martin and Cheshire dropped their marker accurately on the main factory building, then carried out a number of low level passes at just 20ft above the factory. Although putting themselves, their aircraft and crews at risk from ground attack, they were keeping their part of the bargain in making sure that no French civilians were killed in the attack. Their plan worked and all the French workers ran out of the factory to safety, before the aircraft of 617 Squadron dropped their bombs. There were no French civilians killed as a result of the raid.

Four nights later, 617 Squadron tried again. This time it was the Antheor railway viaduct which ran between Saint-Raphael and Nice on the southern coast of France. It was a strategic target as it was a line well used by the Germans to move their military supplies to Italy where they were fighting the Allies. This time their attempt to achieve a similar result failed miserably. The Germans had beefed up their ground defences around the area of the viaduct, and because of this Cheshire couldn't get anywhere near the viaduct to lay his marker, despite making several runs at it. Next it was Martin's turn to try and drop a marker, but he fared even worse. His aircraft was badly struck by flak, which killed the bomb aimer and injured several other crew members, including Martin. On top of this, two of the aircraft's engines were put out of action, and Martin knowing full well that he wasn't going to make it back to England, just about made it back to the safety of an Allied airfield in Sardinia.

Between 2 March and 10 April Cheshire and the other members of 617 Squadron flew eight further missions, perfecting their new marker system. This allowed Cochrane and Cheshire to meet with Harris a second time, who was suitably impressed, but wanted a success against a more heavily defended target, before he was prepared to give Cochrane and Cheshire the twin-engine Mosquito aircraft they so dearly sought to be able to take their achievements to another level. What Harris had in mind was Munich. A German city that he felt hadn't been attacked as much as it should have been up to that point in the war.

Harris told Cochrane and Cheshire that they could have the loan of four Mosquito bombers for the mission, and that their job was to successfully mark Munich's railway yards, for 5 Group to follow them in and bomb them heavily. Do that, and they could have the Mosquitoes that they wanted.

Although up for the challenge set them by Harris, it was far from straightforward, and one that left little room for error. The distance between London and Munich is just over 570 miles as the crow flies, meaning a return journey of 1,140 miles. This meant flying over German-occupied France and Belgium, as well as large swathes of Germany itself to get to Munich. So besides a potential fuel issue, as the return journey would certainly push the Mosquitoes to their operational limits, there was the added and more dangerous aspect of having to fly over numerous locations, where German anti-aircraft batteries would be eagerly waiting to shoot them out of the sky.

When Cheshire briefed his crews about the forthcoming Munich raid there was utter disbelief as the realisation of the sheer scale of what they were up against fully sank in. Allowing for a total of three minutes flying time over the target, they would only have sufficient fuel to get them to Munich and back, plus fifteen minutes further flying time. The raid went ahead on the night of 24/25 April 1944.

After what was a successful raid on Munich, more targets followed, but not all of those raids were successes. The very next one not only didn't go according to plan but also highlighted the issue of successes achieved on the raid, weighed up against the losses sustained by the RAF to get the job done. Let me explain.

The target in question was a Panzer training camp to the north of Paris at a place called Mailly-le-Camp. The raid took place on 3/4 May 1944. Cheshire, flying one of Harris's loaned Mosquitoes led the marking raid for the 346 Lancaster bombers from 1 Group and 5 Group, to follow in behind and carry out the bombing. The raid saw 161 buildings in the camp destroyed and the Germans' 102 vehicles which included 37 tanks; along with 374 casualties, 218 of whom were killed.

British losses were forty-two Lancaster bombers. With seven-man crews for each aircraft it meant they lost 294 men on just one raid, 76 more than German soldiers lost on the ground that night.

Cheshire's skill and that of his colleagues in No. 617 Squadron was brought to the fore on the night of 5/6 June 1944: the night before the Allied landings on the beaches of Normandy. They weren't sent to Normandy, instead they made the short journey across the English Channel to the Pas de Calais region of France, to carry out a spoof raid to make the Germans believe the invasion of occupied Europe had already started, and to remove any belief they might have had that the real target was going to be the beaches of Normandy, just a matter of hours later.

Cheshire and the rest of his colleagues of No. 617 Squadron, were understandably disappointed at not being part of the actual D-Day landings in Normandy, but they most certainly played their part. The squadron's aircraft made a number of low level passes over the English Channel and towards the Pas de Calais area, dropping 'window' or chaff with each pass. This had the effect of making the German defenders in Calais believe that a large number of Allied vessels were on their way across the English Channel and heading straight towards them, which they were not.

This ploy by No. 617 Squadron most definitely helped keep large numbers of German troops and equipment in the Pas de Calais area instead of them being deployed to strengthen defences in Normandy. Higher numbers of troops in Normandy would have undoubtedly meant more Allied soldiers would have been killed, and the breakout from the beaches at Normandy would have been made a lot more difficult and might even have failed. Had invasion failed, the war could have continued for years, resulting in thousands more deaths of both military personnel and civilians.

When looked at in these terms it is clear to see the importance of the role that Cheshire and the rest of his colleagues with No. 617 Squadron played overnight on 5/6 June 1944.

Chaff was a radar counter-measure, developed by different nations before the beginning of the Second World War, Britain being one of them. As early as 1937, British researcher Gerald Touch, who was working with Robert Watson-Watt, an early pioneer of radio direction finding and radar technology, made the suggestion that one way of overwhelming or fooling enemy radar systems would be to suspend lengths of wire from balloons or a parachute. Touch believed that if this was done with large enough amounts of wire, it would produce false echoes on an enemy's radar system, leaving them to believe that they were being attacked by a much larger force than they actually were. Reginald Victor Jones, who was a British physicist and scientist, added to the debate by suggesting that it need not be lengths of wire, just aluminium strips. It was the latter which was eventually used, some ten and a half inches in length and about three-quarters of an inch wide, and packed into bundles that weighed one pound. These would then be placed inside an aircraft and deposited whilst flying over an enemy target.

On a normal radar screen in the Second World War, there would have been a circle on the display and if an enemy target appeared, the circle would be broken at the point where the enemy aircraft had been picked up. By using large amounts of tinfoil, the entire circle would be completely fractured, meaning that the radar operator wouldn't be able to distinguish between whether he was seeing a number of enemy aircraft, ships, or whether his radar was being jammed.

Following the invasion of German-occupied Europe from the beaches of Normandy, No. 617 Squadron got on with trying to knock out the reinforced storage sites of the V1 and V2 rockets. They were successful at the sites at Wizernes and Watten, both of which were situated in the Pas de Calais region. Soon after these attacks, there was a slight change of tack, when on 14 June 1944, Cheshire and No. 617 Squadron carried out a daytime attack on German E-Boat sheds at Le Havre which was home to some fifteen E-Boats, which had been active during the Normandy landings, wreaking havoc amongst Allied shipping and amphibious landing craft as they made their way across the English Channel.

For the attack on the E-boat sheds, No. 617 Squadron used Barnes Wallis's newly designed 'Tallboys'. By the time the attack was over all but one of the E-Boats had been damaged beyond repair. For good measure the squadron also bombed German ships in Le Havre harbour, once again with Tallboy bombs. The resulting blast was so powerful that it blew a number of German ships right out of the water, which then landed on the harbour's quayside.

Cheshire certainly didn't take too much in the way of time off from front-line action. Eleven days later he was part of an attacking force that had been tasked with bombing a V1 underground storage bunker at Siracourt, which is situated in the Pas de Calais region. Cheshire's job was once again to mark the target, but by then he had lost his Mosquito aircraft. Because of the precision required to mark an underground target he needed an aircraft that was fast and manoeuvrable. He liked the idea of using a single seater, P-51 Mustang fighter bomber, but knew that there was no way the RAF would provide one for him, despite the fact they were requiring him to carry out such a precision-based mission.

Somehow he managed to convince the United States Air Force to let him have a P-51 Mustang, not just any old Mustang, but a brand new one. So new in fact that it arrived dismantled in a packaging crate on the morning of the day of the intended raid on the facility at Siracourt. Talk about cutting it fine. For the ground crew, putting it together was no doubt one of the most unusual jobs they had ever been requested to carry out. But things weren't much easier for Cheshire. For one, he had never flown a Mustang before, and the last time he had flown a single-seater aircraft was back when he had been undergoing his initial training, and when he climbed into the cockpit to fly it on the mission to Siracourt, that was the first time the aircraft had been flown. Because of the unusual circumstances of the mission, and the condition that the Americans delivered the Mustang in, there had been no opportunity for Cheshire to carry out any test flights on it.

Despite all these issues, Cheshire arrived at the target on time. He marked it accurately, and three Lancaster bomber aircraft each dropped a Tallboy on it. The subsequent explosion was devastating, and the target was totally destroyed.

The mission that everything had led up to previously, finally arrived. The attack on the underground V3 rocket facility at Mimoyecques had taken place, and it was 6 July 1944, exactly one month after the D-Day landings on the beaches of Normandy. Cheshire had certainly trained for the day at Mimoyecques, and he was as prepared as he could possibly be. There was the additional problem of it being a daytime raid, which brought with it, its own set of unique rules, and certainly raised the risk of more aircraft than usual not making it back home. But the raid was a success. Cheshire in his brand new, never-flown-before Mustang P-51 aircraft, accurately marked the target for 617's Lancaster bombers, and they played their part to perfection. Their specially designed Tallboy bombs landed right on the money. The underground caves collapsed and the threat of the V3 rockets was no more.

The night of 7/8 July 1944 was a significant landmark for Cheshire. The occasion was an attack on the limestone caves at St-Leu-d'Esserent, a location in the north of France the Germans used for the storage of their V1 and V2 Rockets. The raid was also Cheshire's hundredth mission, and the completion of his fourth tour, and although he didn't know it at the time, it was to be his last with Bomber Command. Once again, because of Cheshire's pinpoint marking of the target, and 617's accurate bombing, the mission was a success.

It was soon afterwards that he was informed he was to be awarded the Victoria Cross. Not like many of those who had gone before him, for one act of bravery, or a few acts of selfless gallantry over the course of a battle, but for more than four years of almost continuous bravery that had become a common standard for him.

He was presented with his Victoria Cross by King George VI at Buckingham Palace, but walked forward together with RAF Warrant Officer Norman Jackson, who was also awarded the VC that day for his part in a bombing raid on Schweinfurt in Germany in April 1944.

The saying goes, 'all men are born equal in the eyes of God'. Even if that is the case, there was still something special about Cheshire, something which set him apart from nearly all other men. At his own admission, he had been afflicted with luck and good fortune, but there were two aspects to Cheshire as a man that made him stand out. As an individual, he was either fearless, or just knew how to control his nerves very well indeed. He was a man who had the ability to block out the concept of fear. He didn't see difficult situations as 'taking a risk', he just kept calm and did what needed to be done. He just saw what he did as being the normal way to do things.

Because he managed to keep a calmness about himself, he was able to see things clearly, which helped him stay focused. What others might view as being a potentially dangerous scenario, causing them to take time out to think and weigh up the options, with the overriding consideration being safety, Cheshire just went for it as soon as a scenario presented itself. He was of the mind that the longer a man waited to make a decision on what to do, the more confusing and difficult the situation became. Although some may well have viewed him as being 'gung-ho' or having a 'death wish', he simply had a natural instinct for self-preservation, which helped him out of many tight spots, some of which had only become so because he had put himself in a particular situation in the first place.

The war and his participation in it had maybe turned an ordinary man into what he became. The other aspect of his personality that helped set him apart from others was that he was an outstanding leader to the men who served with him, no matter who they were or what position they filled. It didn't matter to Cheshire whether they were part of his flying crew or part of the ground crew, he knew every one of them by name. He would have a cup of tea and a cigarette, and move from discussing technical issues about his aircraft to personal issues and difficulties that his men might be experiencing.

He was no soft touch either. Although he cared greatly about the wellbeing of his men, there was a war on and they had a job to do, however unsavoury it might be and no matter how difficult it was. If he felt that a pilot just wasn't up to the task at hand, no matter how good a pilot he was, he simply got rid of them.

At the end of the war in Europe, Cheshire was nominated to be one of the official British observers of America's bombing of Nagasaki, the other being a professor of mathematical physics at the Imperial College London. The pair were in a support B-29 bomber named the *Big Stink,* which was later renamed *Dave's Dream.*

Cheshire relinquished his commission and retired from the RAF on 27 January 1946, on medical grounds. The fact that he was somewhat unconventional was borne out, when after the war he established the VIP or *Vade in Pace* or the Go in Peace Colony for veterans and war widows at Gumley Hall in Leicester. From there he moved on to Le Court, near

Petersfield in Hampshire, a mansion which Cheshire acquired from one of his aunts. The aim of the VIP colony was to enable ex-servicemen and women, along with their children, to live together, with the long-term goal of helping them with their transition back into civilian life. The project eventually came to an end in 1947.

In 1948, Cheshire began what is today known as the Leonard Cheshire Disability, which is a charity that supports disabled people and was run from his Le Court property. By the end of the first year, it had twenty-eight patients. The rest of Cheshire's life involved looking after and caring for disabled people.

It would be as appropriate to write a book about Cheshire's post-war life as it would be to write about his wartime achievements. He was quite clearly a truly remarkable human being, who was clearly put on this earth for more than one reason.

Queen Elizabeth II mentioned Cheshire personally in her Christmas message of 1992. In a poll that named Britons top 100 greatest ever individuals, he was number 31 on the list. In 2017, the Roman Catholic Diocese of East Anglia announced that they were putting forward the name of Leonard Cheshire for canonisation as a saint. A better legacy any man could not wish for, especially one who had spent five years of his life during the Second World War witnessing death so closely.

Chapter Five

Thomas Frank Durrant

Thomas Frank Durrant was born on 17 October 1918 in Farnborough Kent. Just a normal child born into a normal working-class family. He attended the local primary school, where he received a basic education. By the time he left he could read and write, add up, multiply and subtract. He couldn't speak Latin, knew nothing about politics, nor matters appertaining to business. But Thomas Durrant certainly had an appetite for hard work. He started his working life as a butcher's boy, making deliveries on a bicycle.

His military career began before the outbreak of the Second World War, when he enlisted in the Corps of Royal Engineers as Private 1874047 on 1 February 1937. With the war less than a year old, Prime Minister Winston Churchill ordered the formation of specially trained troops to carry out hit and run raids on enemy coastline. All individuals who liked the sound of becoming part of this new unit had to volunteer. So it was in 1940 that Thomas Durrant volunteered for service with the Combined Operations Special Independent Companies and after being accepted he was posted to No. 2 Special Independent Company, which had been formed from elements of the 53rd Welsh Division. Many of the units who were part of the division were from the Territorial Army, and went on to be involved in the Norwegian Campaign which lasted between 9 April and 6 June 1940. It was during that time Durrant was promoted to the rank of sergeant.

There were eleven Special Independent Companies (SIC), and it was the first five companies which sailed to Norway in May 1940, under the somewhat intriguing name of 'Scissors Force' to join up with the British Expeditionary Force. Each of the companies were made up of 21 officers and 268 men from the other ranks.

The SIC were an extremely short-lived entity, and by the end of 1940 they had already ceased to exist. But by February 1941 what had once been the Special Service Battalions had become Commando Units. No. 2 Commando was born out of 'B' Company, 1st Special Service Battalion, under the command of Lieutenant Colonel Newman.

Durrant served with No. 1 Commando, at which time there were six in total, and each commando had six troops – one being a heavy weapons troop, which included nine Vickers machine-gun detachments and nine 3-inch mortar detachments. Each of the troops consisted of sixty-five men, consisting of a four-man headquarters unit and two sections, each of thirty-one men. Each of the commando units selected their own officers and men to start with. These were elite units who selected only the very best of those who volunteered. Men who were totally different from the average soldier in a normal infantry unit.

Admiral Sir Roger Keyes was initially the man placed in overall command of the unit, in June 1940, but was replaced by Admiral Louis Mountbatten in October 1941, when he 'resigned,' or was rather removed from his position for coming up with one too many impractical ideas, as far as the chiefs of staff were concerned.

The disciplines they trained in were many. There was a big emphasis on physical fitness, and, in no particular order, they conducted training in survival, orienteering, close-quarter combat, silent killing, signalling, amphibious and cliff assaults, motor-vehicle operations, weapons and demolition. Most ordinary soldiers serving in infantry regiments might have been sufficiently trained in just one of those disciplines, whereas commandos had to be proficient in all of them.

Many of the commandos, especially non-commissioned officers and instructors, attended numerous courses at different locations across the country, although Scotland was where many of these camps tended to be. There was the Special Training Centre at Lochailort, which had set up 'home' in Inverailort House, a building requisitioned by the War Office in May 1940, and trained individuals in the techniques of guerrilla and irregular warfare, along with other 'useful' techniques that might just come in handy for commando units. It was used for different military purposes all the way through until January 1945, when it was handed back to the owner, sadly, not in the same state that it had been in when it was requisitioned by the War Office.

There were other similar training facilities near Inveraray on the west coast of Scotland, some 75 miles from Edinburgh, and at Achnacarry Castle, near Spean Bridge, where there is a monument to commandos who were killed during the Second World War. All training was carried out with live ammunition, to help make the training as realistic as possible.

United We Conquer
IN MEMORY OF THE OFFICERS AND MEN
OF THE COMMANDOS WHO DIED IN THE
SECOND WORLD WAR 1939-1945
THIS COUNTRY WAS THEIR TRAINING GROUND

No. 1 Commando was formed on 13 June 1940, but just six weeks later on 27 July 1940 it became part of No. 1 Special Service Battalion, before once again becoming No. 1 Commando on 5 March 1941, and it was based at Dartmouth.

The night of 27/28 September 1941 saw No. 1 Commando, which included Durrant, take part in Operation Chopper, a raid centred on Saint-Aubin-d'Arquenay in the Calvados region in north-west France. After spending a day there, they left.

The raid on St Nazaire, Operation Chariot, took part on the night of 27/28 March 1942, and was a British amphibious attack on the German-occupied and heavily defended dry docks at St Nazaire on the west coast of France.

The raid was a joint effort on the part of the Royal Navy and British commandos, under the overall command of Combined Operations. The reason for the attack was to put the dock out of use, because without it, any large German warship that needed repairs would have to return to Germany to have the work carried out, forcing them to sail via the English Channel, or what is known as the GIUK gap, which is an acronym of Greenland, Iceland and the United Kingdom, the gap being the open waters between these three islands. This would not have been good for any partly stricken German naval vessels, as this was an expanse of water heavily patrolled by vessels of the Royal Navy.

The British destroyer HMS *Campbeltown*, which had first been launched on 2 January 1919, as USS *Buchanan*, before being transferred to the Royal Navy on 9 September 1940, crossed the English Channel in company with eighteen smaller British vessels. When they all reached the Atlantic coast of France, they made their way up the Loire River, and *Campbeltown* was rammed into the gates of the dry dock. The German defenders would have thought the British action futile, as once the vessel had been removed the dry dock would once again be useable. What they didn't know was *Campbeltown* was packed with a large amount of delayed action explosives, which actually detonated later that day whilst German soldiers were on board examining the vessel. The subsequent explosion damaged the dry dock so badly that it was out of action until 1950.

So the purpose of the *Campbeltown* is clear. But what of the eighteen smaller vessels? Their role was to convey the commandos back to England once the raid had been completed, but many of them were put out of action, set ablaze or sank following up behind the *Campbeltown*, as she made her way up the Loire River.

The commando force, which landed to manually destroy other structures at the dry dock, quickly realised that they were not going to be escaping via the same route they had taken to get there. Instead they fought their way across town to try and make good their escape by land, but eventually had to surrender when they ran out of ammunition. Of the 611 officers and men who had left Falmouth, 168 were killed, 215 were captured and taken as prisoners of war, and the remaining 228 made it back home. A total of eighty-nine of the men who took part in the raid received some kind of gallantry award, this included five Victoria Crosses, one of which was the one earned by Thomas Frank Durrant.

No. 1 and No. 2 Commandos had made their way across the English Channel on motor launches, whilst men of No. 3 Commando were on board HMS *Campbeltown,* under the watchful eye of Captain Hodgeson.

The men from No. 1 Commando had been tasked with securing the Old Mole. This was where those on board the motor launches were expected to land, and it was the point from where all those who survived the action would leave.

One of the small vessels that took part in the raid was HM *Motor Launch 306*. On board was Sergeant Durrant, who by the end of the action would show just how determined an individual he was, but it also showed the ethic and ethos of all the commandos, in their determination to get the job done.

As ML306 made its way towards the Old Mole it came under intense and heavy fire from shore-based German defences, set up to protect the dry dock from a coastal, sea-borne approach. This involved elements of the 280th Naval Artillery Battalion, who had twenty-eight guns of different calibres at their disposal. Alongside them were the additional guns and searchlights of the 22nd Naval Flak Brigade, and in support of these units were soldiers from the 333rd (Wehrmacht) Infantry Division, whose main purpose was to defend the coast line between St Nazaire and Lorient.

How good the British intelligence for the operation was is unclear, but besides the destroyer *Jaguar*, the Germans also had a minesweeper, along with an armed trawler, patrolling along the Loire estuary. Based permanently within the same port area were the 6th and 7th U-boat submarine flotillas, and the 16th and 42nd Minesweeper flotillas were also berthed in the basin on the night of the raid, along with two tanker ships.

The German defensive fire was so intense that ML306 was unable to land its complement of commandos and had to beat a hasty retreat, but whilst making its way back down the Loire River, it came face to face with the German destroyer *Jaguar*, which was coming from the opposite direction. Sergeant Durrant was in charge of a twin Lewis gun that was located on the deck of ML306, and didn't wait to take action, opening fire on his much bigger opponent at the earliest opportunity. The *Jaguar* quickly returned fire, and in no time at all Durrant had already been badly wounded. By the time the *Jaguar* had neutralised the threat from ML306, Durrant lay on her deck suffering with wounds to his head, both arms, both legs, chest and stomach. German sailors took him to a military hospital in St Nazaire, where he died of his wounds the following morning. He was buried at the Escoublac-la-Baule War Cemetery, about 7 miles from St Nazaire.

Once the men of No. 1 Commando had completed their objective of securing the Old Mole and eliminating the Germans' defensive anti-aircraft units, they were to make their way into the old town and blow up a power station, a number of bridges, and the new entrance into the locks.

A week after Durrant's death, the commander of the German destroyer, Kapitanleutnant F. K. Paul, met the commanding officer of the commandos, Lieutenant Colonel Newman, who by then was in a prisoner of war camp in Rennes. Paul approached Newman and informed him of Durrant's heroic actions, going as far as suggesting that the colonel might wish to recommend Durrant for a bravery award of the highest order.

The subsequent citation for Durrant's Victoria Cross, which wasn't officially announced in the *London Gazette* for more than 3 years on 15 June 1945, included the following:

> For great gallantry, skill and devotion to duty when in charge
> of a Lewis gun in HM Motor Launch 306 in the St Nazaire
> raid on 28 March 1942.

Motor Launch 306 came under heavy fire while proceeding up the River Loire towards the port. Sergeant Durrant, in his position abaft the bridge, where he had no cover or protection, engaged enemy gun positions and searchlights ashore. During this engagement he was severely wounded in the arm but refused to leave his gun. The Motor Launch subsequently went down the river and was attacked by a German destroyer at 50 to 60 yards range, and often closer. In this action Sergeant Durrant continued to fire at the destroyer's bridge with the greatest of coolness and with complete disregard of the enemy's fire. The Motor Launch was illuminated by the enemy searchlight, and Sergeant Durrant drew on himself the individual attention of the enemy guns, and was again wounded in many places. Despite these further wounds he stayed in his exposed position, still firing his gun, although after a time only able to support himself by holding on to the gun mounting.

After a running fight, the Commander of the German destroyer called on the Motor Launch to surrender. Sergeant Durrant's answer was a further burst of fire at the destroyer's bridge. Although now very weak, he went on firing, using drums of ammunition as fast as they could be replaced. A renewed attack by the enemy vessel eventually silenced the fire of the Motor Launch, but Sergeant Durrant refused to give up until the destroyer came alongside, grappled the Motor Launch and took prisoner those who remained alive.

Sergeant Durrant's gallant fight was commended by the German officers on boarding the Motor Launch. This very gallant non-commissioned officer later died of the many wounds received in action.

The investiture of the medal took place on 29 October 1945 at Buckingham Palace, when the king presented Durrant's medal to his mother. It is now on permanent display at the Royal Engineers Museum, Prince Arthur Road, Gillingham, Kent.

The following article about Durrant's bravery appeared in the *Birmingham Daily Gazette* dated Wednesday 20 June 1945.

Sergeant Durrant was in charge of a Lewis gun in a motor launch in the raid. Without cover or protection he engaged enemy gun positions and searchlights on shore, and when severely wounded in the arm, refused to leave his post.

The launch was subsequently attacked by a German destroyer at 50-60 yards range and less. Durrant continued to fire at the destroyer's bridge with complete disregard of the enemy's fire.

Illuminated by the enemy searchlight, Durrant drew on himself the individual attention of the enemy guns and was again wounded in many places. He stayed on, firing from his exposed position although after a time only able to support himself by holding on to the gun mounting.

Called on to surrender, Durrant's answer was a further burst of fire at the destroyer's bridge. Now very weak, he went on firing, using drums of ammunition as fast they could be replaced. The enemy eventually silenced the motor-launch, but Durrant refused to give up until the destroyer came alongside and took prisoner those still alive.

His fight was commended by the German officers as they boarded the motor launch.

Another article about Durrant's heroic's appeared in the *Western Morning News,* dated the same day.

Two heroes of the Commando raid on St Nazaire in March 1942, and a Sepoy who nearly became a priest, but joined the Indian Army instead, are awarded the Victoria Cross, it was announced in last night's *London Gazette.*

Lieutenant Colonel Augustus Charles (Gus) Newman, of the Essex Regiment, captured while leading the St Nazaire raid, and repatriated only a few weeks ago, is one of the Commando heroes.

The second, Sergeant Thomas Frank Durrant, Royal Engineers, did not live to learn of his decoration. He died from wounds received as he stuck to his machine gun throughout a running battle between his motor launch and a German destroyer in the mouth of the Loire River.

It is strange to note that despite having been awarded his Victoria Cross for his actions on the night of 27/28 March 1942, it was not officially announced until Tuesday 19 June 1945, three years and three months after the events. Although in Durrant's case the weight of the evidence to support his award came from German officers who witnessed his actions as they fought against him. It would appear that it was only when Lieutenant Colonel Newman was released from his captivity as a prisoner of war and an account was taken from him, that the award to Durrant could be confirmed. Likewise with Newman, it would have been that men who had been captured with him, would have been able to give testimony as to his actions, for his Victoria Cross to be awarded.

Durrant's Victoria Cross was also unusual, maybe even somewhat unique, in that it was the only such award given to a soldier whilst he was involved in a naval action.

Lieutenant Colonel Newman said of Durrant:

> His was a very plucky action. Durrant manned a gun on his launch, and for a mile after mile during the engagement blazed away at the enemy vessel. He was well-nigh dead when the Germans eventually captured the small launch. The Germans took him into St Nazaire, where he died next day in hospital.

Without doubt Durrant was an extremely brave individual.

A man who didn't flinch at carrying out his duty, even though he knew that he had the option to surrender, he chose not to, and instead he decided to open fire on the much larger German destroyer, knowing full well what the consequences of his actions would likely be his own death. But for him there was a bigger picture, the success of the overall operation, of which he was a part. History has recorded that Thomas Durrant most certainly played his part that day, and he will never be forgotten for the price that he was prepared to pay.

A truly remarkable individual, who as a result of his involvement in the Second World War, achieved greatness, and a place in history for ever more. But he did not set out to gain personal acknowledgement, it was just something that he was destined to achieve, because of the type of human being that he was.

Above left: Major Charles Heaphy (1867). 1st VC awarded to a non-regular soldier and also a 1st to a New Zealander.

Above right: Brigadier Milton Fowler Gregg. His VC, awarded during the First World War, was stolen in 1978 and to this day has never been recovered.

Above left: Noel Godfrey Charvasse. Winner of the Victoria Cross twice during the course of the First World War. His 2nd award was posthumous.

Above right: Headstone of Noel Godfrey Charvasse. Brandhoek New Military Cemetery Belgium.

Above left: Filip Konowal. His Victoria Cross, was stolen from the Royal Canadian Regiment Museum in 1973 and was returned in 2004.

Above right: Charles Davis Lucas depicted on the deck of HMS *Hecla*. His was the first ever Victoria Cross awarded in 1854.

Above left: Mrs Elizabeth Webber Harris (1869). Gold Victoria Cross.

Above right: Premindra Sing Bhagat Victoria Cross. (*Creative Commons Attribution-Share Alike 3.0*)

Above left: Leonard Cheshire, Victoria Cross, 1943.

Above right: The Investiture of Charles Pickard, William Blessing and Leonard Cheshire, at Buckingham Palace 28 July 1943.

Above left: Memorial to Leonard Cheshire and Sue Ryder.

Above right: Headstone for Noel Charvasse at Brandhoek New Military Cemetery, Belgium.

Above left: Thomas Frank Durrant.

Above right: Motor Launch similar to one used by Durrant when he was awarded his Victoria Cross.

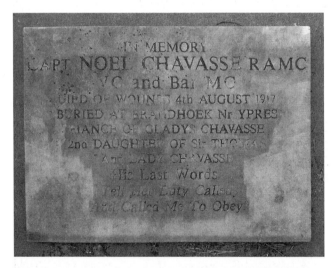

Memorial at Bromsgrove Cemetery to Noel Chavasse. (*Creative Commons Attribution-Share Alike 3.0 Unported*)

Noel Chavasse Memorial on display at the Army Medical Services Museum in London.(*Creative Commons Attribution-Share Alike 3.0 Unported*)

Above: Noel Chavasse's medal collection.

Right: John Wallace Linton (1943).

Above left: Memorial at Falmouth to those lost in the St Nazire raid. (*Thomas Frank Durrant*)

Above right: Guy Gibson's gravestone in Steenbergen, Holland 1944.

Above left: Guy Penrose Gibson in posed photograph in 1944.

Above right: Guy Penrose Gibson in doorway of Lancaster Bomber, No. 617 Squadron May 1943.

Above: Stanley Hollis Memorial in Middlesborough. (*Creative Commons Attribution-Share Alike 4.0 International*)

Left: Memorial to Stanley Hollis on the side of 2 Hollis Crescent, Strensall, North Yorkshire. (*Creative Commons Attribution-Share Alike 4.0 International*)

Above left: Stanley Hollis 1944.

Above right: John Hollington Grayburn (1944).

Above left: James Joseph Magennis (1945).

Above right: Belfast Memorial to Magennis.

Above left: Charles Groves Wright Anderson (1942).

Above right: Edward Colquhuin Charlton (1945).

Above left: John Alexander Cruickshank (1944).

Above right: James Joseph Magennis having just received his VC (1945).

Chapter Six

John Hollington Grayburn

Five men were awarded the Victoria Cross during the Battle of Arnhem, four of which were posthumous awards, and one of those was 26-year-old Lieutenant 149002 John Hollington Grayburn, 2nd Battalion, Parachute Regiment. John Grayburn was born on 30 January 1918, during the final year of the First World War, on Manora Island, India, but his family moved back to England when he was just a young boy. Between 1931 and 1935, he attended the prestigious Sherborne School in Dorset. Founded in AD 705, it was an independent boarding school for boys. After leaving school, he went to work for the Hong Kong and Shanghai Banking Corporation, which today is more commonly known by just its initials, HSBC.

He was initially commissioned as a second lieutenant into the Oxfordshire and Buckinghamshire Light Infantry Regiment in September 1940. He was further promoted to the rank of lieutenant in 1942, but bored with the non-activity of being stationed on the home front, he applied to the Parachute Regiment, and in June 1943 he was accepted and transferred to the 7th (Light Infantry) Parachute Battalion, before later transferring to the regiment's 2nd Battalion, where he was put in command of 2 Platoon, A Company. The battalion's commanding officer was Lieutenant Colonel John Frost.

The Battle of Arnhem in Holland, took place between Sunday, 17 and Monday, 25 September 1944, and was part of Operation Market Garden. After having swept through France and Belgium in the summer months of 1944, the Allies were preparing to enter Holland. This came about as a result of Field Marshal Montgomery wanting the British Second Army to attack the Ruhr, which was the industrial heartland of Germany, but avoiding the heavily defended German Siegfried Line.

The British 1st Airborne Division had landed at Arnhem by both parachute and gliders, along with elements of the 1st Polish Parachute

Brigade. As with all such operations, things didn't quite go according to plan with the landings at Arnhem, for two reasons. Firstly, the bulk of the force didn't land exactly where it was intended to do so. In fact they landed some distance away from their objectives.

Secondly, they encountered unexpected resistance in the form of the 9th and 10th SS Panzer Divisions, which intelligence had not picked up on. This meant that many of the troops, who it was expected would be at the Arnhem Road Bridge, were instead held up on the outskirts of the town fighting with German defensive units. The plan was for the airborne forces to hold the bridge until they were joined by the Allied XXX Corps. Once again this was part of the operation that did not go according to plan, and those at the bridge were overrun by German forces before they could be relieved.

By the end of the fighting, the British 1st Airborne Division had lost 1,174 officers and men who had either been killed in action or died of their wounds, with a further 5,903 who had either been captured or were missing in action. This was out of a total starting force of 8,969, meaning that only 1,892 managed to escape. The Glider Pilot Regiment, who had started out with 1,262 officers and men, saw only 532 of them safely withdrawn. As for the Polish Brigade, they fared much better, only sustaining 203 casualties out of 1,689 officers and men.

This helps provide an overview of what Lieutenant John Hollington Grayburn, found himself a part between 17 and 20 September 1944, at Arnhem.

Major General Roy Urquhart, who was the commanding officer of the 1st Airborne Division, originally selected the 2nd Battalion to lead the 1st Parachute Brigade into Arnhem to secure the road, rail and pontoon bridges over the lower Rhine. In fact it was the battalion's A Company that was chosen to head the march from the drop zone to the bridges at Arnhem. The men of A Company didn't have to wait too long to see action, as they ambushed a small German recce group, not that far from the drop zone. As the men moved off it was decided that the platoons would take turns to lead the march.

Lieutenant Grayburn arrived at the road junction just as he and his men suddenly came under heavy German fire, but despite his precarious situation, Grayburn was not perturbed. Rather than back off he went on the offensive. He got his men to lay down a smoke screen, then led them in an attack that saw them overrun the German positions.

Although there were numerous German patrols in the area, A Company suffered no more delays on their way to the bridge. It was C Company who were in the lead as they finally approached, but before they got too far, German engineers detonated the explosives that they had attached to the underneath of the bridge. In some respects it was a 'godsend' for the men of C Company, because had they arrived just a few minutes earlier, they would have sustained many casualties.

This was one operation which most certainly did not run smoothly, but by 8pm as the day gave way to the early hours of darkness, the men of the 2nd Battalion, 1st Parachute Brigade, were finally in position on both sides of the main ramp, on the northern-most side of the Arnhem Road Bridge. But they wouldn't be getting much in the way of sleep that night.

Once in position, Grayburn decided to ignore the odd German vehicle that was still using the bridge, as he did not want the Germans to be aware of their presence as they awaited the arrival of the rest of their battalion. When Major General John Dutton Frost arrived at the bridge, he set about utilising some of the residential properties that were situated close to the ramp at the northern end of the bridge. At this time it was decided that a small-scale attack over the bridge, towards the German-held, southern side, should be undertaken. It turned out to be a bad decision, as it was easily rebuffed by the German defenders, and wasn't helped by the meagre numbers used in the attack.

When Major Allison Digby Tatham-Warter arrived, who was famous for carrying an umbrella into battle, they tried again, this time with larger numbers. The attack was under the cover of darkness and was led by John Grayburn. To give themselves a better advantage, they blackened their faces and even tried to muffle the sound of their hob-nailed boots, by using strips of curtain, cut from the houses they had been occupying, and attaching them to the underneath of their boots. As the group made it to the bridge they spread out, moving along the girders on either side, but luck was not on their side and they were quickly spotted by the Germans on the other side of the bridge, who had remained alert despite the lull in fighting.

Leading his men in the attempt at crossing the bridge, Grayburn was one of the first hit by enemy fire, when a German bullet struck him in the shoulder. But he just picked himself up, dusted himself down, and got on with the job at hand, that of leading his men. The German defence was spirited to say the least, and it quickly became apparent to Grayburn that to continue would have been suicidal. So intense was the German fire that he made the decision to retreat and get his men to the safety of the British side of the bridge. He was the last one off and back into cover.

It was then simply a case of batten down the hatches, wait for the much-needed reinforcements to arrive, and hope that they did so before the Germans overran them. Some 700 men had made it to the bridge, and every single one of them was needed to help keep the Germans at bay. The men of A Company were holed up in the buildings either side of the bridge that immediately overlooked the river, and were constantly bombarded by the tanks of the 10th SS Panzer Division.

On Tuesday, 19 September, Grayburn led several patrols on and around the area of the bridge. This drew even more German fire and the Germans intensified their attacks gradually, making the British defensive position on the north side of the bridge even more difficult. In part this came about because of German concerns over their own defensive positions on the south side of the bridge, and that the British XXX Corps might break through and capture the bridge from their side. They had become so concerned at this possibility they had laid explosives on a section of the ramp that crossed the road just before the bridge.

In the meantime, Grayburn led a patrol on to the bridge to keep the Germans occupied whilst men from the Royal Engineers removed the fuses from German-laid explosives that had been strategically placed so they could blow up the bridge if they felt that they were going to be overrun by the British. Grayburn was wounded again, but after treatment, and despite having his head bandaged and an arm in a sling, he was quickly back in the thick of it, once again taking charge of his men. Once the Germans saw what the British sappers had done, they sent out some of their men to replace the fuses and charges, whilst laying down covering fire, to keep the British at bay. Not to be deterred, the British sent out another patrol to force the Germans back and remove the fuses for a second time. Yet again Grayburn was wounded, this time in the back, but he refused to leave his men. To try and take control of the situation once and for all, the Germans sent one of their tanks forward, which stopped right next to the position that Grayburn and his men were holed-up in. Realising the precarious position that he and his men were in, Grayburn stood up right in front of the tank, giving his men the time they needed to withdraw. The tank's machine guns opened fire on him almost immediately.

On 20 September, a ceasefire was arranged so that the British could evacuate their wounded, who up to that point were being treated in the cellars of some of the damaged buildings in the vicinity of the bridge. By now the British were getting low on both the number of able-bodied men still capable of carrying on fighting, and ammunition to be able to fight with. The remaining British soldiers were finally overrun in the early hours of 21 September, after having held out for nearly five days.

Major Digby Tatham-Warter had been wounded, captured, and taken as a prisoner of war, but managed to escape from a German hospital. He eventually teamed up with the Dutch resistance, and eventually made it back to England, with well over 100 escaping British soldiers as part of Operation Pegasus, and it was upon his return that a report he wrote about Grayburn's heroics, saw him posthumously awarded the Victoria Cross and promoted to the rank of captain. Tatham-Warter was himself awarded the Distinguished Service Order.

The full citation for Grayburn's Victoria Cross appeared in a supplement to the *London Gazette* dated 23 January, 1945.

> The King has been graciously pleased to approve the posthumous award of the Victoria Cross to:
>
> Lieutenant John Hollington Grayburn (149002), Parachute Regiment, Army Air Corps (Chalfont St. Giles) for supreme courage, leadership and devotion to duty.
>
> Lieutenant Grayburn was a platoon commander of the Parachute Battalion which was dropped on 17th September, 1944, with the task of seizing and holding the bridge over the Rhine at Arnhem.
>
>   North end of the bridge was captured and, early in the night, Lieutenant Grayburn was ordered to assault and capture the Southern end with his platoon. He led his platoon on to the bridge and began the attack with the utmost determination, but the platoon was met by a hail of fire from two 20 mm. quick firing guns, and from the machine guns of an armoured car. Almost at once Lieutenant Grayburn was shot through the shoulder. Although there was no cover on the bridge, and in spite of his wound, Lieutenant Grayburn

continued to press forward with the greatest dash and bravery until casualties became so heavy that he was ordered to withdraw. He directed the withdrawal from the bridge personally and was himself the last man to come off the embankment into comparative cover.

Later, his platoon was ordered to occupy a house which was vital to the defence of the bridge and he personally organised the occupation of the house.

Throughout the next day and night the enemy made ceaseless attacks on the house, using not only infantry with mortars and machine guns but also tanks and self-propelled guns. The house was very exposed and difficult to defend and the fact that it did not fall to the enemy must be attributed to Lieutenant Grayburn's great courage and inspiring leadership. He constantly exposed himself to the enemy's fire while moving among, and encouraging, his platoon, and seemed completely oblivious to danger.

On 19th September, 1944, the enemy renewed his attacks, which increased in intensity, as the house was vital to the defence of the bridge. All attacks were repulsed, due to Lieutenant Grayburn's valour and skill in organising and encouraging his men, until eventually the house was set on fire and had to be evacuated.

Lieutenant Grayburn then took command of elements of all arms, including the remainder of his own company, and reformed them into a fighting force. He spent the night organising a defensive position to cover the approaches to the bridge.

On 20 September 1944, he extended his defence by a series of fighting patrols which prevented the enemy gaining access to the houses in the vicinity, the occupation of which would have prejudiced the defence of the bridge. This forced the enemy to bring up tanks which brought Lieutenant Grayburn's positions under such heavy fire that he was forced to withdraw to an area farther North. The enemy now attempted to lay demolition charges under the bridge and the situation was critical. Realising this, Lieutenant Grayburn organised and led a fighting patrol which drove the enemy off temporarily, and gave time for the fuses to be removed. He was again wounded, this time in the back, but refused to be evacuated.

Finally, an enemy tank, against which Lieutenant Grayburn had no defence, approached so close to his position that it became untenable. He then stood up in full view of the tank and personally directed the withdrawal of his men to the main defensive perimeter to which he had been ordered.

He was killed that night.

From the evening of September 17th until the night of September 20th, 1944, a period of over three days, Lieutenant Grayburn led his men with supreme gallantry and determination. Although in pain and weakened by his wounds, short of food and without sleep, his courage never flagged. There is no doubt that, had it not been for this officer's inspiring leadership and personal bravery, the Arnhem Bridge could never have been held for this time.

After his death, Grayburn's body was recovered and buried on the bridge embankment close to where he had been killed. His remains were recovered in 1948 and reburied at the Arnhem Oosterbeek War Cemetery in the Gelderland region of Holland. Grayburn is one of 1,526 Allied servicemen buried in the cemetery.

He was a married man, and his widow, Dorothy Grayburn, lived in Helensburgh, in Dunbartonshire.

Chapter Seven

Guy Gibson

Guy Gibson was born in Simla, the capital and largest city in the northern Indian state of Himachal Pradesh, on 12 August 1918, just three months before the end of the First World War.

His parents were Alexander and Lenora Gibson, and the family were in India because Alexander's job was with the Imperial Indian Forestry Service, where he rose to become the Chief Conservator of Forests for the Simla Hill States in 1922.

Guy Gibson returned to England in 1924 when he was just 6 years old, along with his mother, elder brother Alex, and his sister Joan, when his parents separated. This must have been an extremely difficult time for Gibson emotionally. Here was a young boy who had only ever known a life in India, suddenly having to deal with the break-up of his parents, whilst also being forced to move to England, a country of which he had very little knowledge, and had never even previously been to.

To make matters even worse, in the years immediately after returning to England, Gibson's mother, Lenora, began drinking heavily, which eventually resulted in her becoming an alcoholic. Her entire personality changed, which resulted in her displaying some very strange behaviour, including being violent to her three children. To counter this, his school helped greatly by finding him lodgings during the school holidays, and later on his aunt and uncle on his mother's side took him in and gave him his own room, which was a big help to both Guy and his mother.

When Gibson was just 14 he found himself in the same class at St Edward's School in Oxford, as someone else who would go on to become a well-known wartime pilot, Douglas Bader.

Academically, Gibson didn't excel. He was just an average boy, who wasn't bottom of the class, but he did rather like science and photography. Even in sport, although he enjoyed playing rugby, it was only ever in the second team. He was however an avid reader, especially in the genre of English history through the ages.

It had always been his ambition as a child to learn how to fly and become a pilot. Like many kids of his era, he had grown up reading about the endeavours of the brave Allied pilots of the First World War. His particular favourite was Albert Ball, who had been awarded the Victoria Cross for his wartime exploits. But it wasn't a life in the military that he yearned for. He wanted to be a civilian test pilot, an idea that he was so set on, that he wrote to aircraft makers, Vickers. His reply came from their chief test pilot, Captain Joseph Summers. His advice was simple, 'join the Royal Air Force on a short term commission'. That's exactly what Gibson did, but after going along for his interview, his application was rejected because he failed his medical. He applied a second time, passed his medical, and commenced a short service commission in late 1936.

There was an irony between Summers and Gibson making contact with each other, as during the Second World War, Summers became a supervising RAF fighter tester, specifically for No. 11 Group RAF, and in preparation of the Dambusters raids of May 1943, Summers was the test pilot for the experiments carried out near Portland in Dorset for the bouncing bombs dropped by Vickers' Wellington aircraft. He had acquired the prestigious position due to the fact that he was a close friend of the bomb's designer, Barnes Wallis.

Gibson's initial pilot's course began on 16 November 1936, at the Bristol Flying School at Yatesbury, Wiltshire. Because of poor weather the course didn't finish until 1 January 1937. The next stage of his training saw him move on to RAF Uxbridge with No. 24 Training Group, where he underwent his basic RAF training. On successful completion of his course he was commissioned with the rank of acting pilot officer with effect from 31 January 1937. He then underwent further training at RAF Netheravon, before he was awarded his pilot's wings on 24 May 1937. With future civilian work in mind, Gibson chose to specialise in the world of multi-engine bomber aircraft and underwent additional training at the No. 3 Armament Training Station at Sutton Bridge, in Lincolnshire. His instructors had noted that Gibson could be rude and condescending to those of a lower rank than himself, in particular the men who were part of the ground crews. This was not a good trait for a pilot of a bomber crew to display, as team work was everything. For a bomber crew that didn't just mean those on board the aircraft, it also included the ground crew, who were an extremely important part of the team, because if they didn't do their job properly, there was chance that something catastrophic could happen to an aircraft in flight. He obviously still had a great deal to learn about being an officer and a gentleman, and how to work as part of a team, no matter what part of the team you were in.

Nine months from start to finish. The same training today (2019) would be somewhere in the region of six years. But then aircraft of the late 1930s were nowhere as near as complicated and intricate as they are today.

Sadly, it would appear that Gibson had not taken on board his instructors' comments about his attitude towards the ground crews, as he was no different at his first posting with No. 83 (Bomber) Squadron, who were stationed at RAF Turnhouse, on the outskirts of Edinburgh. His lack of humility towards others earned him the nickname of 'Bumptious Bastard'. Remember at the time, he was still only 19 years old, and it is likely that the mechanics and ground crews who looked after the squadron's Hawker Hind aircraft, were more than five or six years older than he was.

The next couple of years leading up to the outbreak of the Second World War saw No. 83 Squadron moving about the country. They moved from RAF Turnhouse to RAF Scampton in Lincolnshire. From there they went to RAF Leuchars in Fife, then on to RAF Hemswell in Lincolnshire, RAF Rauceby, also in Lincolnshire, RAF Evanton near Invergordon and RAF Hamble, near Southampton.

In October 1938, Gibson was found guilty of negligence at a Court of Inquiry, in relation to a taxiing incident at RAF Hemsworth.

He was due to leave the RAF sometime in May 1939, but was kept on because of the outbreak of hostilities in Abyssinia. The following month he was promoted to the rank of flying officer.

As the likelihood of war grew, so the level of preparation and readiness increased, resulting in No. 83 Squadron taking part in Home Defence exercises in and around the London area.

With the outbreak of the war on 3 September 1939 Gibson undertook his first operational tour when as part of No. 83 Squadron, he was one of the pilots selected to take part in an attack on the German fleet, which was at anchor at Wilhelmshaven.

On 13 November 1940, Gibson became commander of 'A' Flight, No. 29 Squadron, stationed at RAF Digby in Lincolnshire. At the time the squadron was going through a period of change, both with personnel and aircraft. This wasn't an easy time for Gibson, as he was a 'new boy' brought in to replace the previous under-performing flight commander, which didn't make him particularly popular amongst some of the more experienced pilots. In July 1941 he was awarded a Distinguished Flying Medal and in December the same year he was awarded a Bar to his Distinguished Flying Cross. It was around this time that he was rested from operations and sent to RAF Cranfield as chief flying instructor with No. 51 OTU. In March 1942, Gibson was appointed commanding officer of No. 106 Squadron of Bomber Command, which saw him move to RAF Coningsby in Lincolnshire. Throughout 1942 Gibson's operational flying continued, and in November that year he was awarded the Distinguished Service Order. On 16 January 1943, Gibson had an extra crewman on a night time operation to Berlin. None other than the BBC's distinguished war correspondent, Major Richard Dimbleby. This was a busy time for Gibson and his colleagues, during which time he was awarded a second Bar to his Distinguished Flying Cross and a Bar to his Distinguished Service Order, having completed 172 sorties

After the decision to attack the Ruhr dams had been taken, the man selected to be responsible for the operation's overall planning, preparation and execution was Air Vice Marshal Ralph Cochrane, acting officer commanding No.5 Group. The name put forward as the commanding officer of the squadron who would undertake the mission, was Guy Gibson. On 19 March 1943 he attended a 'meeting' at the headquarters of No. 5 Group, where he was officially informed he would be commanding a new squadron that would be required to carry out a mission that required low flying at night, and had to be executed by 19 May 1943, at the latest. At the meeting he was introduced to Group Captain John Whitworth, the commanding officer of RAF Scampton, where the new squadron would be based.

Initially it was stipulated that the new squadron had to be formed by volunteers from tour-expired crews, although this was later changed to crews that had to have completed or nearly completed two tours of operations. Once again they had to be volunteers.

Gibson arrived at RAF Scampton on 21 March 1943, the same day that the men who would form the ground crews also began to arrive. They had all arrived by the week's end and were inspected to make sure that they were up to scratch, and hadn't just been sent along because other squadrons and RAF stations were taking an opportunity to off load some of their 'dead-wood'. The aircrews began arriving from 24 March, the same day that Gibson went to meet Barnes Wallis at Burhill near Weybridge. For some inexplicable reason, Gibson had not been given a full security clearance, which meant that Wallace was unable to fully brief him on all aspects of the operation and the intended target location. Wallace had adapted a depth charge that was usually dropped from the rear of a ship when searching for enemy submarines. For what Gibson was being tasked with doing, the bombs had to be dropped from a certain height so as to rotate with backspin, whilst the aircraft was travelling at a specific speed. If all of these factors were correct then the bomb would bounce across the surface of the water before striking the intended target.

On 27 March, Gibson was provided with more information about his forthcoming operation but still he wasn't given all the facts, just the details and information of where they would be conducting their training. Most of these were bodies of water or reservoirs at different locations around the country.

No. 617 Squadron began training for the operation at the beginning of April 1943, using Lancaster bomber aircraft that had been specially adapted to carry their bouncing bombs.

The process of selecting crews didn't run totally smoothly, as under Gibson's watchful eye, some crews just simply didn't come up to scratch, and at least one of the crews decided to leave after they learnt that their navigator was deemed to be unsatisfactory. Bomber crews by nature tended to be extremely superstitious, and saw sudden and unexpected changes as a bad omen.

Air Vice Marshal Cochrane arrived at RAF Scampton on 15 May to inform Gibson that the operation he and his men had been training for had arrived, and that it would take place the following evening, over 16/17 May 1943. After the meeting, Whitworth informed Gibson that his pet dog 'Nigger' a black Labrador retriever had been run over by a car and killed. Barnes Wallis was particularly worried as he didn't see the loss of the dog as a good sign, especially as the dog had been the squadron's mascot.

The subsequent attack on the Eder and Möhne dams was a success and the objective was achieved. The Möhne was the first of the dams to be attacked and Gibson's was the lead aircraft, although his bomb missed its target. The next aircraft was flown by Hopgood, but with the German defenders now on high alert his was always going to be a difficult run into the target. Hopgood's aircraft was struck by anti-aircraft units, caught fire and blew up, but the crew had managed to release their bomb before doing so. This also missed. Next up was Harold Morgan 'Micky' Martin, who would later become Air Marshal Sir Harold Martin. His bomb also missed. Then it was the turn of Young, his bomb was the first success of the raid, although his triumph wasn't immediately obvious. It was only when Squadron Leader David Maltby began his run that it was apparent to everybody that Young's bomb had breached the dam. It was just before 1am on 17 May 1943 that Hutchinson gave the code word 'Nigger', the name of Gibson's recently killed dog, over the radio to the headquarters of No. 5 Group, which was the confirmation that the Möhne dam had been breached.

Next came the Eder dam. Neither of the bombs dropped by Shannon or Maudslay breached the dam. Next to try his luck was Knight. His bomb successfully breached the dam just before 2am. Hutchinson gave the same code word for the breaching of the Eder dam and repeated it, before all the surviving aircraft turned and made for home.

The success of the attack came at a heavy cost. Eight aircraft were lost along with a total of fifty-six crew. On Sunday, 20 May 1943, whilst away with his wife on weekend leave, Gibson received a telephone call informing him that he had been awarded the Victoria Cross. It was a bittersweet moment for him, as he couldn't help but think of all those who had not made it back, many of whom he had recruited and trained for the mission.

King George VI and the Queen visited RAF Scampton on 27 May, where they had lunch in the officers' mess, inspected the squadron and were shown charts, maps and photographs of the area of the dams, and some of the very aircraft that had carried out the raid.

Gibson met the queen for a second time, less than a month later on 22 June 1943, when she presented him with his Victoria Cross and a Bar to his Distinguished Service Order at an investiture at Buckingham Palace.

On 4 August 1943, Gibson set sail on board the Queen Mary as one of the party accompanying the Prime Minister, Winston Churchill, en route to the Quadrant Conference in Quebec, Canada. After the conference he stayed and undertook a two-month tour of Canada and the United States, before returning home on 1 December 1943.

Afterwards there was a brief dabble with politics, when he was selected as the Conservative prospective candidate for Macclesfield, followed by a staff course at the RAF's Staff College at Bulstrode Park in Buckinghamshire.

By the middle of July 1944 he was back flying operationally once again. On 19 September 1944 the Royal Air Force was ordered to carry out an attack on Bremen in Germany. Gibson was one of those who took part in the raid, flying a Mosquito B.XX *KB267i* which took off from its base at RAF Coningsby just before 8pm. Within two hours they had arrived at their target location, dropped their bombs and had started their return flight to the UK. What happened to the aircraft is still a mystery. What is known is that Gibson's aircraft crashed at Steenbergen in Holland at about 10.30pm on 19 September 1944. Back home in England there was no great panic about Gibson's initial no-show, mainly over the confusion about where he had landed. When he didn't arrive at Woodhall Spa it was just assumed that he had landed at Coningsby instead, and because of the foggy weather the control tower there simply assumed that he had landed elsewhere. But after everyone had been accounted for, it soon became apparent that he had not returned from the mission.

Suggestions have been put forward that Gibson's aircraft was shot down by German anti-aircraft units; that it was shot down by German fighter ace, Kurt Welter, although this was later proved to be incorrect. It has been suggested that it ran out of fuel, and even that it was shot down by friendly fire. Rear Gunner, Sergeant Bernard McCormack, who also took part in the raid, passed away in 1992. On his death he left a taped confession stating that he believed that he was actually responsible for shooting down Gibson. He stated that in the skies over Steenbergen, he saw what he believed to be a German Junkers Ju 88 aircraft, and fired some 600 rounds at it, after which he saw the aircraft go down. This account was witnessed by another of the Lancaster crews who were also part of the raid. It was only the next day when it was realised that Gibson hadn't returned and McCormack was informed that there had been no Junkers aircraft in the area at the time, that it dawned on him what he had probably done.

Even with death being the obvious consequence of war, the loss of a highly decorated pilot was a major blow, one that could be felt far and wide across the nation and have a negative effect on morale. The Prime Minister, Winston Churchill, wasn't informed until 26 September, and Gibson was not officially reported as being missing until 29 November. His death was formally announced on 8 January 1945.

At the crash site at Steenbergen, the remains of both Gibson and his navigator, Squadron Leader Jim Warwick, were found. The Dutch gave the two men a good funeral, even down to providing a wonderful horse-drawn carriage and the coffin was draped in a Dutch flag. As it wasn't known by the local townsfolk what religion either of the men were, the funeral was taken by both a Roman Catholic priest and a Protestant Pastor. A cross with the names of both men on it was erected over the grave at the Steenbergen-en-Kruisland Roman Catholic Cemetery in Holland.

It has to be said that despite his early negative attitude towards ground crew, he really was an incredible individual. During the Second World War, approximately 55,000 British pilots and crews were killed in raids over Europe, making it an extremely dangerous military role. This wasn't helped by the fact that in the early months of the war, British bomber crews flew day time missions, which meant that they were easy prey for the fast-moving and manoeuvrable German fighter aircraft. Some of those 1939 day-time missions ended badly for so many of the crews. It wasn't uncommon for some of them to lose more than 50 per cent of the aircraft that set off.

The feeling of dread amongst bomber crews must have been at a very high level. What it must have felt like to be approaching a target, as the aircraft was picked up by enemy searchlights and then fired upon by anti-aircraft batteries, can only be guessed at. An aircraft, still carrying a large amount of fuel, fully laden with its bomb payload, whilst being fired at by anti-aircraft guns, must have tested the resolve of many a good man.

A British bomber crew had to fly thirty missions before they had completed a single tour, and before they were placed on the training wing. But to have a mission counted towards a tour the crew had to take a photograph as proof of having bombed their target. Without this photograph, the mission wouldn't count towards the tour.

Gibson undertook somewhere in the region of 180 wartime missions, meaning that he had survived the equivalent of six 30-mission tours, when many of the air crews didn't even survive half the number of flights required to complete just one tour. This all went to show just how remarkable a young man Gibson was. It has to be remembered that he flew all those flights, was awarded all his gallantry medals, and at the time of his death he was still only 26.

Below is the citation for Gibson's Victoria Cross, as released by the Air Ministry.

The King has been graciously pleased to confer the Victoria Cross on the undermentioned officer in recognition of most conspicuous bravery:

Acting Wing Commander Guy Penrose Gibson, DSO, DFC (39438), Reserve of Air Force Officers, No. 617 Squadron.

This officer served as a night bomber pilot at the beginning of the war and quickly established a reputation as an outstanding operational pilot. In addition to taking the fullest possible share in all normal operations, he made single-handed attacks during his 'rest' nights on such highly defended objectives as the German battleship, *Tirpitz*, then completing in Wilhelmshaven.

When his tour of operational duty was concluded, he asked for a further operational posting and went to a night-fighter unit instead of being posted for instructional duties. In the course of his second operational tour, he destroyed at least three enemy bombers and contributed much to the raising and development of new night fighter formations.

After a short period in a training unit he again volunteered for operational duties and returned to night bombers. Both as an operational pilot and as a leader of his squadron, he achieved outstanding successful results and his personal courage knew no bounds. Berlin, Cologne, Danzig, Gdynia, Genoa, Le Creusot, Milan, Nuremberg and Stuttgart were among the targets he attacked by day and night.

On the conclusion of his third operational tour, Wing Commander Gibson pressed strongly to be allowed to remain on operations and he was selected to command a squadron then forming for special tasks. Under his inspiring leadership, this squadron has now executed one of the most devastating attacks of the war, the breaching of the Moehne and Eder dams.

The task was fraught with danger and difficulty. Wing Commander Gibson personally made the initial attack on the Moehne dam. Descending to within a few feet of the water and taking the full brunt of the anti-aircraft defences, he delivered his attack with great accuracy. Afterwards he circled very low for 30 minutes drawing the enemy fire on himself in order to leave as free a run as possible to the following aircraft which were attacking the dam in turn.

Wing Commander Gibson then led the remainder of his force to the Eder dam where, with complete disregard for his own safety, he repeated his tactics and once more drew on himself the enemy fire so that the attack could be successfully developed.

Wing Commander Gibson has completed over 170 sorties, involving more than 600 hours operational flying. Throughout his operational career, prolonged exceptionally at his own request, he has shown leadership, determination and valour of the highest order.

Gibson was also awarded the Legion of Merit (Commander) by the President of the United States of America. This was announced by the Air Ministry on 3 December 1943. He had also been awarded the Distinguished Flying Cross and Bar in 1940 and 1941, respectively, as well as the Distinguished Service Order and Bar in 1942 and 1943.

It was clear to see that Gibson wasn't awarded the Victoria Cross for one definitive act, but numerous different ones, some of which had also been included in the other gallantry awards that he had received.

Perhaps the best words written as an epitaph to Guy Gibson, were those of the inventor of the bouncing bomb, Barnes Wallis.

For some men of great courage and adventure, inactivity was a slow death. Would a man like Gibson ever have adjusted back to peacetime life? One can imagine it would have been a somewhat empty existence after all he had been through. Facing death had become his drug. He had seen countless friends and comrades perish in the great crusade. Perhaps something in him even welcomed the inevitability he had always felt that before the war ended he would join them in their Bomber Command Valhalla. He had pushed his luck beyond all limits and he knew it. But that was the kind of man he was. A man of great courage, inspiration and leadership. A man born for war, but born to fall in war.

In October 1951 a book written by Paul Brickhill, entitled *The Dam Busters* was published. It told the story not only of the raids on the dams, but all the other incredible things that Guy Gibson and his colleagues at 617 Squadron did during the Second World War, with their last raid being the raid on Hitler's lair at Berchtesgaden. The book included claims that No. 617 Squadron was the most effective unit of its size that Britain ever had.

Part of the book's story looks at the squadron's achievements, which to no small degree were not down to an airman, but to the inventions of an ageing aircraft designer, by the name of Barnes Wallis. The bouncing bomb, the finite breach of the Möhne, Eder and Sorpe dams in Germany. The book also included an in-depth explanation of the purpose of the Tallboy bombs and how they were used to prevent Hitler's V1 and V2 rockets from wreaking havoc on London and a number of other UK cities. Not forgetting that it was the Wallis and 617 Squadron combination that sank the German naval vessels, the *Tirpitz* and the *Lutzow*.

After the end of the war, the Royal Commission on Inventions awarded Wallis £10,000, as it recognised his work had materially shortened the length of the Second World War and by doing so had saved thousands of lives. But rather than spend it on himself, he gave it to an educational trust at Christ's Hospital in conjunction with the RAF Benevolent Fund, which went towards helping to educate children of men who had died whilst serving in the RAF. In giving the money so freely, he quoted 'David' from the bible in Samuel II; Chapter 23: *'Is not this the blood of the men that went in jeopardy of their lives?'* To quantify the quote he added that the finest bombs that had ever been invented would be useless without young men like Gibson and his colleagues, who were of sufficient courage to fight through determined enemy defences to drop them, and had sufficient skill to be able to do so with pinpoint accuracy.

As far as Wallis was concerned, all the men of 617 Squadron were both young enough and courageous enough to be able to carry out such attacks. He used the long list of decorations that the men of the squadron had been awarded throughout the war as evidence of that, which was headed by the Victoria Crosses of Gibson, and his successor, Leonard Cheshire.

Wallis had been deeply affected by the Dambusters raid, and the bravery shown by Gibson and his fellow airmen who took part in it.

Nineteen aircraft took off from the UK to take part in the raid. Fifty-five men and eight aircraft, never made it back. Paul Brickhill's book was full of brief accounts of the men of 617 and how they conducted themselves during battle. One story spoke of a low-level attack that was carried out on the Dortmund Ems canal. One of the aircraft had two engines out and was getting shot to pieces, when the pilot, who was close to death, calmly said over the radio to his squadron leader, 'Two port engines gone. May I have permission to jettison the bomb?' Nothing further was ever heard from the pilot or his aircraft.

So good was the accuracy of the men of 617 Squadron that they could drop bombs on a factory and leave the canteen and surrounding houses intact.

When looking back at what Guy Gibson achieved and was involved in during the Second World War, it is incredible that when he led the attack on the Möhne and Eder Dams, he was only 24. He wasn't just one of the men who took part in the raid, he was the commanding officer of No. 617 Squadron, and led his men on the raid.

How did a man of such tender years possess such nerves of steel? At the time of his death, aged 26, he had been flying for five years, and met his end whilst flying a Mosquito over Holland on what was his 175th sortie. What it must have been like for him to squeeze into the tight frame of the cockpit of a Lancaster Bomber, or similar aircraft, time after time, and then disappear into the night skies on a bombing mission somewhere over German-occupied Europe, can only be guessed at.

Some men only flew on a small number of flights before being shot down and killed. For others, their luck held out and they made it through to the end of a tour of thirty missions, but Gibson somehow managed to complete nearly six tours worth of flights, and it was only on that last mission that his luck ran out.

The thirty missions to complete a tour milestone had a caveat attached to it, and that was for crews of No. 8 (Pathfinder Force) Group. Within that group were specialist squadrons, whose job it was to mark targets for the main attacks of Bomber Command. The men who flew with these squadrons had to complete a tour that consisted of a staggering forty-five missions. But there was a sensible reason for this. To become a proficient 'target marker' required a lot of training and practice. There were some who would complete the required forty-five missions, and simply carry on rather than stop operational flying.

Gibson as a pilot was ultimately not just in charge of the aircraft that he was flying but also responsible for the lives of all his crew, a massive responsibility, especially for someone as young as Gibson. Including himself, each Lancaster Bomber had a crew of seven. There was the pilot, Gibson, who would sit in the left hand seat in the cockpit. Seated next to him, but in a collapsible seat, was not, as you might imagine, a co-pilot, because there was no co-pilot, but the flight engineer. Immediately behind Gibson, but facing towards the left side of the aircraft, was the navigator. The bomb aimer fulfilled two roles: that of the front turret gunner, but when operating as the bomb aimer, he was in a laying position adjacent to the bomb bays. The wireless operator would be seated next to the navigator but facing to the front of the aircraft. The mid-upper gunner was situated somewhere in the middle section of the aircraft, and in essence firing out of the top of the fuselage. The rear gunner was perhaps the bravest man on the aircraft, and not a position anybody would wish to be in if they were claustrophobic. It was certainly an isolated position, as once in there was no coming out until the mission was over and the aircraft had returned to base. A rear gunner would more than likely not see any of their crew mates for the entire period of time the mission took to fly.

Some of the aircraft used for Pathfinder missions had an additional crew member. He was also a navigator, but would be used as a radar operator.

When you see photographs of the inside of a Lancaster bomber, with a full complement of crew, it looks absolutely packed, with no room to spare at all.

As if a reminder was needed to show just how brave these young men were, remember that all these men were volunteers. Not one of them were conscripted personnel.

Gibson was a married man, his wedding to Eve Moore took place on 23 November 1940, in the Anglican Church at Penarth, Wales. He was 22 years old and Eve was seven years his senior at 29. They had first met in December 1939, when she was appearing in a revue at the New Hippodrome Theatre in Coventry as a dancer and actress. Because of their work, they weren't always together, which can be a problem for some couples, especially during a time of war. They last met at the time of Gibson's twenty-sixth birthday, with rumours abounding that one of the topics of discussion was about getting divorced, although they never did. There were no children from the marriage.

Chapter Eight

Stanley Hollis

Given the acts of extreme bravery carried out by many men on D-Day landings of 6 June 1944 it is remarkable that only one Victoria Cross was awarded as a result of their actions. That recipient was Stanley Elton Hollis, a truly remarkable individual who rightly deserves to be included in this book. The fact it was the only Victoria Cross awarded that day goes someway to showing just how incredibly brave Hollis's actions were, as there were undoubtedly many men who landed on the beaches of Normandy on 6 June whose courageous actions were deemed only worthy of a Distinguished Service Order or a Distinguished Conduct Medal, Military Cross or Military Medal.

One of the many acts of bravery on D-Day was that of Sergeant Austin 'Bobby' Joyce, of the 1st Battalion, Welsh Guards, who led his platoon in an attack on a heavily defended farmhouse, where he shot a German gunner, threw a hand grenade through an open window, and captured the remaining twenty-six German soldiers who were inside the farmhouse in. For his act of bravery he was awarded the Military Medal. He was later promoted to the rank of major and in 1952 was awarded the MBE.

Stanley Hollis was born on 21 September 1912 in Middlesbrough in the North Riding of Yorkshire. His father, Albert, had a fish and chip shop, and along with his mother Edith, they lived in a flat above the shop.

Stanley didn't shy away from a fight even as a child, he wasn't a bully, but he stood up for himself whenever the circumstances determined that he should do so. For most kids back then, that's just how life was. It was a simple part of growing up. It was what a boy was expected to do. When compared with how harsh life could be for most working-class families, having to stand up for yourself was not an alien concept to them.

Joining the army had not always been the focus of Stanley's attentions. In 1929 he became an apprentice with the Whitby Shipping Company and trained to be a navigation officer. The opportunity to go off and see parts of the world he could have only otherwise dream about, was a great opportunity for a kid from a northern industrial town. But sadly for him, his maritime career was destined to be short-lived. During the course of his apprenticeship he made many voyages backwards and forwards across the seas to West Africa, and in 1930 he became ill when he contracted Blackwater Fever, a form of malaria that can lead to kidney failure and in extreme cases, death.

So it was, at the tender age of 18, Stanley sadly discovered at first hand that life wasn't always fair, and that for him there was not going be a life on the ocean wave. Instead, with his dream of enjoying a maritime life shattered, he returned to dry land and became a lorry driver, which must have felt very mundane by comparison.

In 1939, with the threat of war imminent, Stanley, like many of his peers, wanted to do his bit for king and country. This was his time, and he didn't want to miss out on a piece of the action. There were not too many men who looked forward to a time long after the war was over, and their grandchildren were asking them what they had done during the war, only to reply they hadn't been part of it.

So it was with all these thoughts swirling round inside his head that he enlisted in the 4th Battalion, Yorkshire Regiment (Green Howards) which was a territorial unit. When the Second World War began in September 1939, Stanley, who was nearly 27, was mobilised and transferred to the regiment's 6th Battalion, and went to France as part of the British Expeditionary Force in early 1940. His first job was as the dispatch rider for the regiment's commanding officer, and was promoted to the rank of lance corporal.

He had only been in France for about four months when the British Expeditionary Force, along with French and Belgian forces had been pushed all the way back to the French coastline by rapidly advancing German forces. It was a strange turn of events. One minute the BEF had advanced rapidly into Belgium, as far as the River Dyle, but then German forces had broken through further south as a result of defeating French forces at the Battle of Sedan, which took place between 12 and 15 May 1940. This immediately placed the Allied army groups that were in Belgium in danger, because with the French defeated at Sedan they had very little in the way of protection on their flank.

The Germans knew that if they moved quickly and aggressively enough, they would be able to entrap large numbers of Allied troops before they could reach the French coast. Even then, as far as most observers of the time would have believed, with the English Channel to their backs, the Allied forces would have two choices, either surrender, or fight a rear-guard action on wide expanses of open beaches that offered very little in the way of cover. If either scenario had unfolded, it could have quite easily been the end of the war for Britain. As it was, during the mass evacuations at Dunkirk, Britain lost a huge amount of equipment and vehicles, left behind to make good their escape. In the circumstances, a small price to pay.

Stanley was one of those who made good his escape from the French coastline, and was brought back safely to England from Dunkirk. He was promoted to sergeant during the actual evacuation. After a period of recuperation, Stanley joined the British Eighth Army, and served with them as they fought their way across North Africa. This included the two Battles of El Alamein, the first of which took place between 1 and 27 July 1942, and the second which lasted from 23 October to 11 November 1942. The total number of casualties sustained by the Allies over both battles was more than 26,000. He also saw service during the Battle of Tunisia that lasted between 17 November 1942 and 13 May 1943, where the Allies sustained a further 76,000 casualties, but which ended in a resounding Allied victory, and saw the final defeat of Germany and the other Axis nations in North Africa.

The Allied invasion of Sicily began on 9 July 1943 and continued through until 17 August 1943. It was just before the invasion that Stanley Hollis was promoted to the rank of company sergeant major. It was during the fighting in Sicily that Hollis was wounded at the Battle of Primosole Bridge. It was for his actions during this battle that he was put forward for the Distinguished Conduct Medal but the recommendation was never approved.

The Primosole Bridge was a solidly built structure made of steel girders. It had a total span of 400ft, and crossed over the Simeto River. The job of defending the bridge was in the hands of the Italians, and to help them do just that, two pillboxes had been built on both the north and south sides of the bridge, which had highway 114 passing right through it.

The land to the north of the bridge consisted mainly of olive and almond groves in the surrounding fields, which were prominently overlooked by three big hills that were situated on the south side of the bridge.

On D-Day, the 6th and 7th battalions, Green Howards landed on Gold Beach on the Normandy coast. 'Gold' was the code name for the middle of the five nominated attack areas, and stretched from Port-en-Bessin on the west, to La Rivière in the east. The objective for those landing on Gold was to secure a beach head, before moving west to capture the French town of Arromanches and meet up with American forces who had made their way inland from Omaha Beach. From there they would capture Bayeux and the small coastal port of Port-en-Bessin, before meeting up with Canadian forces from Juno Beach.

Coming ashore on Gold Beach, Stanley Hollis and his colleagues found themselves up against elements of the German 352nd Infantry Division along with soldiers from the German 716th Infantry Division. In total there were about 2,000 German defenders waiting to try and throw the Allied forces back into the sea.

Even though many of Hollis's men would have been experienced fighters, others were young and it would have been their first time in battle, so part of his job on the way to the beach in the landing craft would have been to reassure them and try to keep them relaxed. Some would have been asking him questions, others praying, whilst others would have been talking about their families. Although Hollis cared about those under his command, as long as his men were focused on the job at hand, he wasn't too bothered what they were thinking about.

The Commonwealth War Graves Commission website records that the Green Howards lost a total of twenty-nine men on D-Day, and six of these were only aged 19. Young men, all of whom would have only just finished their basic training after enlistment, before finding themselves right in the thick of the fighting in what history would record as one of the most monumental days ever.

After the initial landings his company moved tentatively inland from the beaches, which wouldn't have been an incident-free transition, with the entire area being raked by German machine guns. At a certain point the company came to an enforced halt, whilst Hollis and his company commander went ahead to investigate two German pillboxes at the Mont Fleur battery which had previously been bypassed. As they drew nearer to the first of the two pillboxes, a burst of fire came from the first of the German positions, but luckily neither Hollis nor his commanding officer were hit. Without any hesitation or instruction to do so, Hollis rushed towards the first of the structures, firing his Sten gun as he went. His speed and daring won the day and he took all but five of the German occupants prisoner. The shock of this 'mad Englishman' dashing towards their position, whilst displaying absolutely no fear, was enough to make them surrender. He must have appeared to them as being super human as their machine-gun bursts had no effect on him at all. After neutralising the threat posed by the enemy soldiers in the first pillbox, he then turned his attention to the second one, attacking it in a similar robust, and almost carefree manner. His demeanour must have appeared even more frightening, as this time he captured the entire twenty-six German soldiers inside it, who were more than happy to surrender and bring their war to an end.

But Hollis still hadn't finished his day's work. With his aggressive demeanour being displayed to the full, he next cleared a neighbouring enemy trench, by killing a number of the German defenders and capturing the others, who were quick to drop their weapons and raise their hands in surrender to ensure they didn't suffer the same fate.

Hollis was a natural warrior who showed no fear or emotion as he continued to go about his work, no doubt an inspiration to the young soldiers under his command. Later that day, he led an unsuccessful attack on a German position which contained a field gun and a number of MG 42, Spandau machine guns: formidable weapons with an average rate of fire power of 1,000 rounds per minute, effective at up to 2,000 metres, and much further if used with a tripod. After the attack had faltered, Hollis quickly realised that the only sensible option was to withdraw, so as not to incur unnecessary casualties. In doing so he learned that two of his men had been wounded and inadvertently been left behind; a situation that he was keen to rectify. He told his commanding officer that as it was he who took the men in, it was down to him to go back and try to get them out. Taking a grenade from one of his men, Hollis carefully observed the enemy's pattern of behaviour and threw it at the most opportune moment. Unfortunately, he had failed to prime the grenade but the enemy did not know that, and kept their heads down waiting for it to explode. By the time they had realised their mistake, Hollis had reached their position and was on top of them, quickly shooting them all before they could react.

The fighting continued, albeit sporadically, as Allied forces continued to push the Germans eastwards back across France. Paris was liberated on 26 August 1944, allowing the return of General Charles de

Gaulle, who had lead the Free French, from his exile in London. By 16 September 1944, all of France, apart from the far north-east corner of the country, had been liberated. It was during this push in September that Hollis was wounded in the leg and evacuated back home to England.

After he had recovered from his wounds, he was informed that he was to be given an award for his heroics on D-Day. On 10 October 1944, he attended Buckingham Palace with his wife, where he was decorated with the Victoria Cross by King George VI.

The citation for his Victoria Cross, which appeared in the *London Gazette* newspaper on 15 August 1944, read as follows:

> The King has been graciously pleased to approve the award of the Victoria Cross for valour to:
>
> Stanley Elton Hollis of the Green Howards (Alexandra Princess of Wales Own Yorkshire Regiment.)
>
> In Normandy on 6 June 1944, during the assault on the beaches and the Mont Fleur Battery, Company Sergeant Major Hollis's Company Commander noticed that two of the pill-boxes had been bypassed, and went with CSM Hollis to see that they were clear. When they were 20 yards from the pill-box, a machine gun opened fire from the slit and CSM Hollis instantly rushed straight at the pillbox, firing his Sten gun. He jumped on top of the pill box, re-charged his magazine, threw a grenade in through the door and fired his Sten gun into it, killing two Germans and taking the remainder prisoners. He then cleared several Germans from a neighbouring trench.
>
> By his action he undoubtedly saved his company from being fired on heavily from the rear and enabled them to open the main beach exit.
>
> Later the same day, in the village of Crepon, the company encountered a field gun and crew armed with Spandaus at 100 yards range. CSM Hollis was put in command of a party to cover an attack on the gun, but the movement was held up. Seeing this, CSM Hollis pushed right forward to engage the gun with a PIAT from a house at 50 yards range. He was

observed by a sniper who fired and grazed his right cheek, and at the same moment the gun swung round and fired at point blank range into the house. To avoid fallen masonry, CSM Hollis moved his party to an alternative position. Two of the enemy gun crew had by this time been killed, and the gun was destroyed shortly afterwards. He later found that two of his men had stayed behind in the house, and immediately volunteered to get them out. In full view of the enemy who were continually firing at him, he went forward alone using a Bren gun to distract their attention from the other men. Under cover of his diversion, the two men were able to get back.

Wherever the fighting was heaviest CSM Hollis appeared and in the course of a magnificent day's work, he displayed the utmost gallantry and on two separate occasions his courage and initiative prevented the enemy from holding up the advance at critical stages. It was largely through his heroism and resourcefulness that the Company's objectives were gained and casualties were not heavier, and by his own bravery he saved the lives of many of his men.

On Saturday, 18 November 1944, an article in the *Birmingham Daily Gazette,* reported how Company Sergeant Major Stanley Hollis and Lance Corporal Francis Jefferson, of the 2nd Battalion, Royal Fusiliers, both holders of the Victoria Cross, met up with a civilian, Mr Fred Parkes who, it had been announced, was to be awarded the George Medal.

The meeting had come about as the two winners of the Victoria Cross were on a tour of Birmingham. They went to the factory where Piat mortar and bombs were manufactured and where Mr Parkes was a senior charge hand. It was the twelfth such factory, involved in the war effort in some way or another, which had been visited by the two holders of the Victoria Cross. Mr Parkes, of 46 Robert Road, Handsworth, had been awarded the George Medal for his actions on 26 October 1940, whilst working as a warden in the works' ARP organisation.

The premises in question were on fire as a result of being struck by a bomb dropped by the German Luftwaffe, which had caused the factory's high pressure gas main to catch fire. Despite knowing the danger he was placing himself in, Mr Parkes allowed himself to be lowered head first into a cellar, crawled under the burning building, and managed to turn off the gas at the main, so that the firefighters were able to get the fire under control, and extinguish it.

In welcoming Company Sergeant Major Hollis and Lance Corporal Jefferson to the factory, the company's managing director remarked that in time of war it was heartening to know that the nation possessed men of brain who were able to design and produce different types of weaponry for the war effort. But for such weapons to fulfil their purpose the country also needed men of valour to put them to the purpose for which they were intended, because if such men did not exist then the finest weapon might just as well be an old broomstick.

In the course of winning their Victoria Crosses, both Hollis and Jefferson had used the Piat to great effect against enemy armoured vehicles. Both men thanked the workers on behalf of the army for helping to produce such a 'wonderful' weapon.

Lance Corporal Jefferson's Victoria Cross was stolen from his mother's home at Luton Street, Bolton, Lancashire during a burglary in 1982. It has never been recovered.

On Thursday, 11 January 1945 an article appeared in the *Dundee Courier* concerning Stanley Hollis, whose status as a holder of the Victoria Cross was being used to its fullest capacity in an effort to boost morale on the home front. The article read as follows:

> CSM Stanley E Hollis, VC, Green Howards, who won his decoration on D-Day for silencing a pillbox single handed, paid tribute to Dundee Jute Mills yesterday for the manufacture of sandbags. He addressed employees of South Anchor Jute Works.
>
> He said that a sandbag to an infantryman was a life saver. Every man carried two with him when going into action to be filled with sand, clay, mud or cement powder in an emergency. He added that a sandbag would stop small arms fire, and it was a very vital part of a soldier's battlefield equipment.

The purpose of such morale-boosting visits by individuals who had been awarded Britain's highest award for gallantry, was that morale came to be recognised as a 'significant military factor, and propaganda emerged as an essential weapon in the national arsenal'. Put into context, Hollis's visit to the Dundee Jute Mills had little to do with sandbags, and everything to do with a large number of Scottish workers getting to see a real live hero: a man who had been awarded the Victoria Cross for his gallantry in battle, and who in doing so had killed enemy combatants. Just seeing such a man made the workers feel better about themselves and more inclined to work harder knowing that their efforts were having a positive effect on the nation's war effort.

And as the war was drawing to its close in Japan, Stanley Hollis was still doing his best to keep up the spirits of the civilian population. Once again he found himself in Scotland doing his bit on the Home Front. An article in the *Aberdeen Press and Journal* dated Monday, 6 August 1945, explained what he was doing.

> CSM Stanley Hollis, the Green Howards VC, thinks the Gordon Highlanders, alongside whom he often fought in North Africa and Europe, are among the grandest fighting men he knows.
>
> 'If you keep up the tradition of the Gordons, you've got something to do,' he told Gordons' ACF boys from city units whom he inspected at Aberdeen yesterday.
>
> 'If you keep up that tradition you'll have justified the training you have taken on,' he added.
>
> The inspection took place at Hazlehead as a prelude to the annual drumhead service arranged by the Aberdeen branch of the British Legion to commemorate the outbreak of the last war.
>
> The service was marred by a freak rainstorm, which drenched hundreds of people in the Hazlehead grounds, while not a drop fell in parts of the West End, less than a mile away.
>
> Rain began to fall as CSM Hollis was inspecting the cadets. People who had gathered at the bandstand enclosure for the service made a rush for shelter. In a few minutes only a handful of people remained seated in the enclosure, while hundreds clustered under the branches of nearby trees. There they stood while they joined in the service, conducted

by the Rev. T J T Nicol, the Aberdeen Chaplain who won the MC while serving with the Eighth Army.

As the steady rain developed into a torrential downpour it was decided to cut the service short.

CSM Hollis, who was to have delivered an address, confined his remarks to thanking the British Legion and the people of Aberdeen for the hospitality which he and his wife had received since they arrived in the city on Friday.

It would appear that the War Office went out of its way to protect winners of the Victoria Cross in the Second World War. Where possible, living recipients were sent on morale-boosting tours rather than back to active operations where they risked being killed. If this was official policy on the part of the War Office, then it was more about the concern for the effect that their death would have on the public morale, than about the individual Victoria Cross winner.

It happened with Hollis and it certainly happened with Guy Gibson, who (in no particular order) was sent on a tour of America and Canada; posted to the RAF's training wing; made a Group Captain, which in effect grounded him; and given a desk job, which turned out to be a cover so that he would have the time to sit down and write a book about his exploits. When they did eventually give in to his request to be allowed to return to operational duties, he was killed in action, but by what now appears to have been a friendly fire incident. On the precept that the War Office knew this to be the case, at the time, they then had to cover that fact up, because if the truth had come out, it could have had a significant negative effect on public morale. If Gibson was actually killed in a friendly fire incident, and was in fact shot down by another RAF aircraft, how sad would that be, that something that Germany and her allies could not achieve, Britain actually did herself.

If that was an agenda in which the War Office participated, it is understandable and makes perfect sense. When these men were awarded their Victoria Crosses they were made to sound like they were super human. Although their actions could be rightly described as being super-human efforts, the men themselves were not. They were ordinary human beings who had carried out incredible feats of bravery, which in many cases were so extreme, it was difficult to understand how they had actually survived the acts they had carried out. But then the criteria for being awarded the Victoria Cross were of such a high standard, men were not expected to survive the actions they had taken to be awarded it in the first place. It was almost a catch 22 situation.

After the war was over and Stanley had left the Green Howards, he returned to his wife Alice (née Clixby) who he'd married in 1933, and children – a son Brian and a daughter Pauline. As a family man, in a social setting he was a relatively quiet individual, not one to make a fuss, and not somebody who was happy talking about his wartime achievements. After the war he had a number of different jobs, which included being a ship's engineer, a sandblaster at a steelworks, and a landlord at two different pubs across North Yorkshire. The first of these was at North Ormesby which he aptly named the Green Howard. Troublesome customers were not something he encountered that much because most people knew who he was. For those who didn't know anything of his wartime achievements and wanted to cause trouble, such encounters didn't last long.

The fact that more hasn't been written about Hollis and his exploits on Gold Beach on D-Day, where he was one of the 60,000 men who landed on 6 June, is largely down the fact that he was fundamentally a modest man. It certainly wasn't down to there being no interest in his story, because there was. It was because his modest perception of himself and what he did as a soldier during the Second World War, was nothing special. It was just him going about his job. That's how he saw himself.

It may be partly because of this that history has focused solely on his winning of the Victoria Cross, but there was more to the man than just that. The clue is his rank. He was a company sergeant major. That is not something that is achieved easily, and it is certainly not a rank that was given to just anybody. It had to be earned, and during the years of the Second World War, and the years immediately leading up to it, one of the only ways of earning it was to consistently display how good a soldier you were, coupled with an ability to be able to lead others, and have them be able to rely on you as well as respect you.

The other aspect that seems to be overlooked, albeit unintentionally is that Hollis and the Green Howards were both battle-hardened, and one of the first on to the beaches of Normandy. Their regimental battle honours for the Second World War were as follows:

Elements of the Green Howards were involved in the Norwegian Campaign between 9 April and 10 June in 1940, as part of the Allied forces who attempted to liberate Norway from the hands of Nazi Germany. The Battle of Arras, which took place on 21 May 1940, also saw men from the Green Howards display courage and bravery of the highest order. Four battalions of the Green Howards, the 4th, 5th, 6th and 7th, had all been sent across the waters of the English Channel in the early months of 1940. The 6th and 7th had only set foot in France on 24 April 1940, and by the end of May, during the Dunkirk evacuations, they were already on their way home to Blighty. Other notable honours were earned during the First Battle of El Alamein which took place between 1 and 27 July 1942. They also saw action during the North African Campaign, during 1942-43; the Battle of Wadi Akarit, over the two days of 6 and 7 April 1943; the Allied invasion of Sicily, between 9 July and 17 August 1943, and subsequent operations throughout Italy during 1943 and 1944, and Burma in 1945.

So, as can be seen, by the time of the D-Day landings on 6 June 1944, they were one of the most experienced infantry regiments in the entire British army, and Stanley Hollis had been with them for nearly every step of the way.

Hollis died on 8 February 1972 at the relatively young age of 59, and he was buried at the Acklam Cemetery in Middlesbrough. Besides his funeral being attended by family and friends, many of his ex-colleagues from the Green Howards, of all ranks, also attended, such was the love and respect that people had for him.

Chapter Nine

James Joseph Magennis

James Joseph Magennis, whose actual surname was, McGinnes, was born in West Belfast, Ireland, on 27 October 1919. On leaving school as a 15-year-old, he enlisted in the Royal Navy on 3 June 1935. After serving on numerous different warships, and in December 1942, with the war in its fourth year, he was drafted into the Royal Navy's submarine service.

A young man who was keen to do his bit, in March 1943, Magennis volunteered for what was entitled 'special and hazardous duties', which in simple terms meant working with midget submarines. Having successfully undergone training as an underwater diver, he took part in his first operation and what also happened to be the first major use of the midget submarines.

In September 1943, two midget submarines, HMS *X6* and HMS *X7*, took part in Operation Source, which saw them penetrate Kafjord, Norway, and disable the German battleship, the *Tirpitz*, which had been located there. For his part in the operation, Magennis was mentioned in despatches 'for bravery and devotion to duty'. He remained with the midget submarines and in July 1945 he was the diver on the midget submarine, HMS *XE3*, which had been tasked, as part of Operation Struggle, with destroying the 10,000 ton Japanese cruiser, *Takao*, at anchor in Singapore harbour.

It was 30 July 1945 when the Royal Navy submarine *Stygian* towed the *XE3* to within some 40 miles of her intended target. From where she slipped her tow to reaching the *Takao*, her journey took her fourteen nerve-wrecking hours to complete, which included passing through minefields and Japanese listening posts en route, which they did without being discovered. The four-man crew must have had nerves of steel to do what they did that day. Being a member of the crew of a full size submarine would, one imagines, require a certain mental approach, more so during a time of war. Sometimes having to spend weeks at a time at sea, under the waves, not knowing if your next breath was going to be your last, was most definitely not for the faint-hearted. To leave that and then become the crew member of a much smaller underwater vessel is, in itself, going far above and beyond a normal level of duty.

The *XE3* came to a stop at 1pm on 31 July 1945. When the moment was right, Magennis climbed out of the midget submarine and swam the short distance to the *Takoa*. Before he could attach any of his limpet mines to the underneath of the ship's hull, he had to chip away at the barnacles, a task which took him some thirty minutes to complete, all the time wondering if he would gave away his presence by the continued noise. Only then was he able to connect all his limpet mines and swim back to the *XE3*.

On getting back on board the midget submarine, he discovered that that one of the side charges, which contained 2 tons of amatol explosive, would not release properly. Without a moment's hesitation, Magennis immediately volunteered to swim out and release it. After several minutes of using a heavy spanner he managed to resolve the problem and returned to *XE3*, which allowed more than enough time for the midget submarine and its four-man crew to safely make their way back to their rendezvous point with the *Stygian*.

Each minute he was in the water must have seemed like an eternity. Was it going to explode while he was working on it? Was he going to be detected by the Japanese before he finished? Was his oxygen going to last long enough? All of these thoughts and more were rushing through his head, whilst he still had to get on and deal with the problem in front of him. The last thing on his mind would have been whether he was going to be awarded a medal or not.

For his actions that day Magennis was awarded the Victoria Cross, the citation of which appeared in the *London Gazette* dated 13 November 1945. It read as follows:

Admiralty Whitehall, 13th November 1945.

The King has been graciously pleased to approve the award of the Victoria Cross for valour to:

Temporary Acting Leading Seaman, James Joseph Magennis, D/JX 144907.

Leading Seaman Magennis served as a Diver in His Majesty's Midget Submarine XE-3 for her attack on 31 July

1945, on a Japanese cruiser of the Atago class. The diver's hatch could not be fully opened because XE-3 was tightly jammed under the target, and Magennis had to squeeze himself through the narrow space available.

He experienced great difficulty in placing his limpets on the bottom of the cruiser owing both to the foul state of the bottom and to the pronounced slope upon which the limpets would not hold. Before a limpet could be placed, therefore, Magennis had to thoroughly scrape the area clear of barnacles, and in order to secure the limpets he had to tie them in pairs by a line passing under the cruiser's keel. This was very tiring work for a diver, and he was moreover handicapped by a steady leakage of oxygen which was ascending in bubbles to the surface. A lesser man would have been content to place a few limpets and then return to the craft. Magennis, however, persisted until he had placed his full outfit before returning to the craft in an exhausted condition. Shortly after withdrawing, Lieutenant Fraser endeavoured to jettison his limpet carriers, but one of these would not release itself and fall clear of the craft. Despite his exhaustion, his oxygen leak and the fact that there was every probability of his being sighted, Magennis at once volunteered to leave the craft and free the carrier rather than allow a less experienced diver to undertake the job. After several minutes of nerve-racking work he succeeded in releasing the carrier. Magennis displayed very great courage and devotion to duty and complete disregard for his own safety.

The XE-class of submarines was a series of midget submarines, which didn't come into service with the Royal Navy until 1944. There had been midget submarines prior to this, but they were part of the original X-class, as had been used in the attack on the German battleship *Tirpitz*.

The XE carried a crew of four which was typically made up of a lieutenant, a sub lieutenant, an engine room artificer, who was there just in case the vessel encountered any mechanical problems, and a seaman or leading seaman, who was usually engaged as the diver. Each vessel usually carried six limpet mines, which would be attached to the hull of enemy shipping by magnets, and weighed about twenty pounds. They also carried two side charges, each containing two tons of amatol explosive. Amatol was a mixture of ammonium nitrate and TNT, and was a highly explosive material.

Some six hours after the limpet mines had been affixed to the Japanese cruiser, *Takoa*, and well after the midget submarine, *XE-3* had left the immediate area, they exploded, ripping a hole in the vessel's hull, which was some 60ft by 30ft in size.

The *Takoa* was not actually seaworthy at the time it was destroyed, due to previous damage caused by a submarine-launched torpedo. The blast also damaged some of the ship's turrets and caused flooding to a number of her compartments. The purpose of the ship's presence at the Singapore's Naval Base, was to protect it from Allied air attacks. It later transpired that the *Takoa* only had a skeleton crew on board, and she was carrying no ammunition for her 8-inch guns, but the British did not know that at the time. The naval base was surrendered by the Japanese to the British on 21 September 1945. Five weeks later the *Takoa* was towed to the Strait of Malacca and sunk as target practice by ships of the Royal Navy.

The following article appeared in the *Belfast Telegraph* on Wednesday, 14 November 1945 concerning the awarding of the Victoria Cross to James Joseph Magennis.

First Ulster VC of the War for Belfast Navy man

A boy who left his home in Belfast at the age of 15½, to join the Royal Navy has won the Victoria Cross for 'very great courage and devotion to duty in complete disregard of his own safety' in a successful midget submarine attack on the Japanese cruiser Takoa, near Singapore in July last. He is Leading Seaman James Joseph Magennis, aged 26 whose mother lives at 8 Ebor Street, Donegal Road, Belfast. His VC is the first to be awarded to an Ulsterman during the war.

Magennis who was the diver, had to force himself out of the hatch, and before he was able to attach his limpet mines to the hull he had to spend 45 minutes with oxygen leaking from his breathing apparatus, scraping off barnacles and seaweed. He was exhausted when he returned inside the submarine, but after a short rest went out again to clear one of the limpet carriers which threatened to upset buoyancy. This was done with a spanner in seven minutes. The submarine XE3 returned successfully from her daring exploit.

Leading Seaman Magennis, who is unmarried, is now serving in HM submarine *Voracious* at Sydney. He went to St Finian's School, Falls Road, where his favourite sport was swimming. He was mentioned in despatches in December 1943. He was last home on leave at that time.

His brother Anthony is also in the Royal Navy, from which another brother, William, has just been demobilised. Mrs Magennis and her daughter, Rosemary, worked on munitions in Bradford for eighteen months.

He corresponded regularly with his mother, but only once did he make a casual reference to the exploit which won him the decoration. He dismissed the action, in these few words; 'We have pulled off a good job, and I expect you will see it in the papers. The pressmen came aboard at Sydney and took our story.'

Mrs Magennis's first action yesterday was to send a cablegram of congratulations to her son.

She is thrilled at the thought of accompanying her son to Buckingham Palace to receive the VC. She smiled wistfully as she added, 'I'll have to be looking my best when we go to see the King, but dear knows where I'll get the coupons for new clothes.'

Neighbours in the Ebor Street district who have now heard the news are already making preparations for an elaborate reception for their sailor VC when he arrives home.

In the same newspaper and on the same day, it was reported that the prime minister of Northern Ireland had sent a telegram to Leading Seaman James Joseph Magennis, congratulating him on the award of his well-deserved Victoria Cross:

Heartiest congratulations on your award of the Victoria Cross. It is the highest honour paid to heroism, courage and devotion to duty. We are all proud of you. – Basil Brooke.

What Magennis's reaction was on having received the prime minister's telegram, was not recorded, although one could guess it was a message that was both well received and appreciated.

An article appeared in the *Northern Whig* on Friday, 23 November 1945 about the instigation of a 'Shilling Fund'.

A Shilling Fund, with a limit of 20 shillings on any individual subscription, is to be opened in Belfast as a citizens' tribute to Leading Seaman James Joseph Magennis, of Ebor Street, Belfast, the first Ulsterman to be awarded the Victoria Cross in the Second World War.

The Lord Mayor, Sir Crawford McCullagh, on whose initiative this decision was taken, will act as hon. treasurer, and the presentation will be made publicly on a date to be arranged.

First steps in the organisation of the Fund were taken yesterday at a meeting convened by the Lord Mayor and held in the City Hall. It was the unanimous feeling of the meeting that the people of the city would desire to mark the award to seaman Magennis of the highest honour for gallantry, and in order that the opportunity of contributing may be afforded to everyone who so desires, it was decided that the movement should take the form of a Shilling Fund, with a limit of twenty shillings on individual subscriptions.

Contributions to the Fund will be received at City Hall. The movement, it is confidently expected, will be popularly supported by workers in city firms, and the Lord Mayor and the committee would be greatly assisted if arrangements were made by the employees in the various works and factories to organise the collection of subscriptions to be forwarded to the Lord Mayor.

The investiture for the award of Magennis's Victoria Cross was carried out by King George VI and took place at Buckingham Palace on Tuesday, 11 December 1945. Also awarded his Victoria Cross at the same investiture ceremony, was Lieutenant Ian Fraser, who was with Magennis on the midget submarine on the attack in Singapore on 31 July 1945.

Magennis was the only individual born in Northern Ireland to be awarded the Victoria Cross during the Second World War, which not surprisingly made him somewhat of a celebrity in his native country, especially amongst the residents of Belfast. In an unprecedented show of respect for a young man who was one of their own, the people of Belfast raised more than £3,000, which would be somewhere in the region of about £60,000 today, as part of that Shilling Fund.

Despite Magennis's wartime heroism and his award of the Victoria Cross, he was not given the Freedom of the City of Belfast. Opinions differ over why this was so. There are some who claim it was down to religious reasons, in a city that was strongly divided by such matters, whilst others point to a class system that couldn't comprehend bestowing such a prestigious award on someone from the inner city slums. Either way, it was a disgusting and ill-considered decision, whoever was responsible for making it. With the benefit of hindsight, those individuals will have known they were wrong. Whether that subsequently ever played on their minds is doubtful.

This in itself is an excellent example of just how winning a Victoria Cross, wasn't always as positive an experience as it should have been for the individuals who were awarded the decoration, especially those who were men from the other ranks. An extreme act of bravery in the face of the enemy, which resulted in a man being awarded a Victoria Cross, won him the respect of his colleagues, all military personnel alike and the general public of a grateful nation. This sadly didn't always equate to a job or financial security once the war was over and they had returned to a civilian life.

Magennis married in 1946, and he and his wife, Edna Skidmore, went on to have four sons. He remained in the navy after the war, not leaving until 1949, when he returned to live in his home city of Belfast, before moving to Yorkshire in 1955. He died in Halifax, West Yorkshire on 11 February 1986, at the age of 66.

Lord Ashcroft purchased Magennis's Victoria Cross for £29,000, soon after his death. This also happens to be the first Victoria Cross that Lord Ashcroft ever purchased. As of May 2018, he owned 213 Victoria Crosses, all of which are on display at the Imperial War Museum in London, and are believed to be worth somewhere in the region of £30 million.

Having it on display in a relevant museum, on a long-term loan would be appealing, and for me, the right thing to do, knowing that in doing so, others would have the opportunity to enjoy it as well.

Chapter Ten

Charles Upham

Charles Upham is one of only three men who have ever been awarded the Victoria Cross twice, and all three of them had the added connection of holding the rank of captain. The other two men were Surgeon Captain Arthur Martin-Leake and Captain Noel Chavasse.

Surgeon Captain Arthur Martin-Leake was first awarded the Victoria Cross as a result of his actions during the Boer War in 1902. He risked his life to treat a soldier who was wounded just 100 metres from the enemy lines. Despite being shot and injured, he continued to treat other wounded soldiers. Before he collapsed of exhaustion, he issued an order that those other wounded officers and men should be given water before he was.

His second Victoria Cross was awarded in recognition of his service in Belgium during the First World War in 1914, where he risked his life rescuing wounded men whilst under fire from enemy guns.

Captain Noel Chavasse was twice awarded the Victoria Cross for his service during the First World War. Before the war, Chavasse had studied medicine at Oxford University and went on to compete in the 400 metres at the 1908 Olympic Games that took place in London.

At the outbreak of the First World War, he was keen to enlist so he joined the Royal Army Medical Corps. His unit was attached to 10th Battalion, King's (Liverpool) Regiment. In 1915 he fought at the Battle of Hooge, which was one of the bloodiest battles of the war. By the end of the battle, the battalion only had 2 officers and 140 men who had survived out of the unit's 900 officers and men who had taken part in the battle.

As a result of the bravery he displayed during the battle, Captain Chavasse was presented with the Military Cross.

On the first day of the Battle of the Somme, Chavasse's battalion was tasked with launching an attack on the fortified village of Guillemont. Not surprisingly the 10th Battalion suffered heavy casualties, with Chavasse working late into the night to tend to the wounded men. On two occasions he was struck by shrapnel and also carried a wounded man across no man's land to the safety of the British trenches. He also tried to collect the dog tags of men who had been killed in the attack.

Chavasse fought at the Battle of Passchendaele in July 1917, during which he manned an advanced first-aid post in a captured German dugout. The Germans shelled this position and Chavasse suffered a blow to the head which fractured his skull. According to a witness, he simply took off his helmet, bandaged his wounded head and carried on with his work, despite suffering two more head injuries as a result of more shelling. Stretcher-bearers took other wounded men to safety on Chavasse's orders, whilst he stayed put. He continued to conduct dangerous searches for other wounded British soldiers. On 2 August 1917 he was severely wounded in the stomach by a shell blast. He died of his injuries two days later on 4 August 1917. He was 32 years old.

Back to Charles Upham and his two Victoria Crosses. In March 1941, Upham and his men left for Greece, but whilst there they had to withdraw and make their way to Crete, which wasn't safe for them either, once large numbers of German paratroopers landed. It was during the subsequent fighting on Crete between 22 and 30 May 1941, when he was wounded in action, that he was awarded his first Victoria Cross.

The citation for this award was announced by the War Office on 14 October 1941.

> The King has been graciously pleased to approve of awards of the Victoria Cross to the undermentioned:
>
> Second Lieutenant Charles Hazlitt Upham (8077), New Zealand Military Forces.
>
> During the operations in Crete this officer performed a series of remarkable exploits, showing outstanding leadership, tactical skill and utter indifference to danger.

He commanded a forward platoon in the attack on Maleme on 22nd May and fought his way forward for over 3,000 yards unsupported by any other arms and against a defence strongly organised in depth. During this operation his platoon destroyed numerous enemy posts but on three occasions sections were temporarily held up.

In the first case, under a heavy fire from a machine gun nest he advanced to close quarters with pistol and grenades, so demoralizing the occupants that his section was able to 'mop up' with ease.

Another of his sections was then held up by two machine guns in a house. He went in and placed a grenade through a window, destroying the crew of one machine gun and several others, the other machine gun being silenced by the fire of his sections.

In the third case he crawled to within 15 yards of an M.G. post and killed the gunners with a grenade. When his Company withdrew from Maleme he helped to carry a wounded man out under fire, and together with another officer rallied more men together to carry other wounded men out. He was then sent to bring in a company which had become isolated. With a Corporal he went through enemy territory over 600 yards, killing two Germans on the way, found the company, and brought it back to the Battalion's new position. But for this action it would have been completely cut off.

During the following two days his platoon occupied an exposed position on forward slopes and was continuously under fire. Second Lieutenant Upham was blown over by one mortar shell, and painfully wounded by a piece of shrapnel behind the left shoulder, by another. He disregarded this wound and remained on duty. He also received a bullet in the foot which he later removed in Egypt.

At Galatos on 25th May his platoon was heavily engaged and came under severe mortar and machine-gun fire. While his platoon stopped under cover of a ridge, Second Lieutenant Upham went forward, observed the enemy and brought the platoon forward when the Germans advanced. They killed over 40 with fire and grenades and forced the remainder to fall back. When his platoon was ordered to retire he sent it back under the platoon Sergeant and he went back to warn other troops that they were being cut off. When he came out himself he was fired on by two Germans. He fell and shammed dead, then crawled into a position and having the use of only one arm rested his rifle in the fork of a tree and as the Germans came forward he killed them both. The second to fall actually hit the muzzle of the rifle as he fell.

On 30th May at Sphakia, his platoon was ordered to deal with a party of the enemy which had advanced down a ravine to near Force Headquarters. Though in an exhausted condition he climbed the steep hill to the west of the ravine, placed his men in positions on the slope overlooking the ravine and himself went to the top with a Bren gun and two riflemen. By clever tactics he induced the enemy party to expose itself and then at a range of 500 yards shot 22 and caused the remainder to disperse in panic.

During the whole of the operations he suffered from dysentery and was able to eat very little, in addition to being wounded and bruised.

He showed superb coolness, great skill and dash and complete disregard of danger. His conduct and leadership inspired his whole platoon to fight magnificently throughout, and in fact was an inspiration to the Battalion.

So Upham's first Victoria Cross wasn't just for a solitary act, but for a number of remarkable acts of selfless bravery, along with the leadership and inspiration of his men throughout. He achieved all this whilst wounded and indisposed with dysentery. For most men, achieving what he had would have been sufficient not only to prove themselves as a 'warrior' but because they had won for themselves, through their unstinting efforts, greatness for eternity.

His second award of the Victoria Cross came about just over a year later, after he had fully recuperated from his wounds received during the fighting on Crete, and been promoted to the rank of captain. This time he was in Egypt and taking part in the fighting at the First Battle of El Alamein.

The citation for his award, news of which had been announced by the War Office on 26 September 1945, appeared in the *London Gazette* dated 14 October 1945, and read as follows:

The King has been graciously pleased to approve the award of a Bar to the Victoria Cross to:

Captain (8077) Charles Hazlitt Upham VC, New Zealand Military Forces.

Captain C H Upham, VC, was commanding a company of New Zealand troops in the Western Desert during the operations which culminated in the attack on El Ruweisat Ridge on the night of 14th - 15th July, 1942.

In spite of being twice wounded, once when crossing open ground swept by enemy fire to inspect his forward sections guarding our mine-fields and again when he completely destroyed an entire truck load of German soldiers with hand grenades, Captain Upham insisted on remaining with his men to take part in the final assault.

During the opening stages of the attack on the ridge Captain Upham's Company formed part of the reserve battalion, but, when communications with the forward troops broke down and he was instructed to send up an officer to report on the progress of the attack, he went out himself armed with a Spandau gun and, after several sharp encounters with enemy machine gun posts, succeeded in bringing back the required information. Just before dawn the reserve battalion was ordered forward, but, when it had almost reached its objective, very heavy fire was encountered from a strongly defended enemy locality, consisting of four machine gun posts and a number of tanks.

Captain Upham, without hesitation, at once led his Company in a determined attack on the two nearest strongpoints on the left flank of the sector. His voice could be heard above the din of battle cheering on his men and, in spite of the fierce resistance of the enemy and the heavy casualties on both sides, the objective was captured.

Captain Upham, during the engagement, himself destroyed a German tank and several guns and vehicles with grenades and although he was shot through the elbow by a machine

90

gun bullet and had his arm broken, he went on again to a forward position and brought back some of his men who had become isolated. He continued to dominate the situation until his men had beaten off a violent enemy counter-attack and consolidated the vital position which they had won under his inspiring leadership.

Exhausted by pain from his wound and weak from loss of blood, Captain Upham was then removed to the Regimental Aid Post, but immediately his wound had been dressed he returned to his men, remaining with them all day long under heavy enemy artillery and mortar fire, until he was again severely wounded and being now unable to move, fell into the hands of the enemy when, his gallant Company having being reduced to only six survivors, his position was finally overrun by superior enemy forces, in spite of the outstanding gallantry and magnificent leadership shown by Captain Upham.

The following information also appeared in the *London Gazette* on 26 September 1945, which covered Upham's second investiture for the Victoria Cross.

Upham had been invested with his first Victoria Cross on 11 May 1945 at Buckingham Palace, by King George VI. When the recommendation was made for Upham to receive a second Victoria Cross, the king remarked to Major General Howard Kippenberger, himself a New Zealander, that a bar to the Victoria Cross would be 'very unusual indeed' and asked him directly, 'Does he deserve it?' Major General Kippenberger replied, 'In my respectful opinion, sir, Upham won the VC several times over.'

Unbeknown to the king, Colonel Burrows had already approached Kippenberger concerning Upham's part in the Mingar Qaim action during the Battle of Mersa Matruh, which took place between 26 and 29 June 1942, which was before Upham's heroics and subsequent capture at the Battle of Ruweisat.

In fact, General Lindsay Merritt Inglis, who in 1942, was the commanding officer of the 2nd New Zealand Division, had received separate citations in relation to Upham's actions at both Mingar Qaim and Ruweisat, which recommended that he merited the award of the Victoria Cross for each of the actions. It would appear that one of the main reasons that he didn't, was because of the king's remarks to Major General Kippenberger, and the rarity of multiple Victoria Crosses being awarded to one man. Ultimately the decision was taken to combine the recommendations for Mingar Qaim and Ruweisat into one. So it is clear to see that if it hadn't been for 'politics', possibly even a lack of backbone on the part of certain individuals, and even a bit of 'snobbery', Upham would have more than likely received a second Bar to his Victoria Cross, making him the singularly, bravest man the Commonwealth and New Zealand had ever seen.

Although Upham was one of only three men to have ever been awarded a Bar to his Victoria Cross, the other two recipients, Martin-Leake and Chavasse, were both non-combatants, in that they served as doctors with the Royal Army Medical Corps and their heroic efforts came in the act of saving the lives of wounded men on the battlefield.

Upham was captured at Ruweisat, taken prisoner of war by the Germans and sent to an Italian hospital for treatment. Having inspected his wounds, an Italian doctor suggested to him that his badly wounded arm needed amputating, mainly because the hospital's medical supplies were scarce due to the war, and if the wound became gangrenous they had no medicines to treat it with. This was a recommendation that Upham immediately turned down, mainly because he had seen other patients at the hospital undergo similar amputations and die during the surgery, screaming in agony because the operations were conducted without anaesthetic. That was not the way he saw himself dying. Fortunately for Upham there was an Allied doctor at the hospital, himself a prisoner of war, who dressed the wound for him. This allowed Upham to remain at the hospital while he recuperated, but despite his wounds and poor physical condition, he still attempted to escape.

One such escape attempt took place whilst he was part of a group of Allied prisoners being transported in a truck. As it slowed for a bend, he jumped and made good his escape, but only managed a distance of about 400 yards before he was recaptured. This wasn't down to the speed in which his captors chased after him, but because he had broken an ankle when he jumped from the moving truck. Once he had recovered from that injury, he wasted no time in trying to escape once again, but there was nothing sophisticated about his attempt. There was no tunnel, no elaborate disguise, he simply walked up to one of the camp's wire fences and climbed up it. When he reached the top he became entangled in barbed wire, before falling to the ground in the space between the two sets of fence. He was immediately surrounded by prison guards, one of whom pointed a pistol at his head and made ready to fire. Upham did not panic or beg for his life, instead he just lit a cigarette and calmly blew rings of smoke into the air. Thankfully for Upham, the guard did not pull the trigger of his gun. The Germans did however snap away with a camera and took pictures of Upham's escape bid.

Because of the number of times Upham had attempted to escape, the Germans classified him as being extremely dangerous and placed him in solitary confinement. He was even made to exercise away from any other Allied prisoners, but whilst being accompanied by two armed guards and with a third armed with a machine gun in a tower. But he had no intention of seeing out the rest of the war in a German prisoner of war camp, regardless of how safe or comfortable it might be. As he saw it, he was a soldier and the Germans were his enemy. On one occasion he ran from his two guards, out of his exercise area, through the adjoining German barracks, and out of the main gates of the camp. Upham was soon recaptured, but this time he had gone too far, and he found himself being sent to infamous Oflag IV-C, which was more commonly known as Colditz. He arrived there on 14 October 1944, and would have arrived there even earlier, but Upham even made another escape attempt on his way to being taken to the castle. His transfer was by civilian train, and he was told that he was only allowed to go to the toilet when the train was travelling at high speed. This was to ensure that he did not try to jump out of the train's toilet window, but a speeding train wasn't going to stop him from escaping, it did however cause him to be knocked unconscious when he jumped from the toilet window and landed on the side of the track below. By the time the guards had discovered he had escaped, the train had travelled on for many miles. A search was begun and some twelve hours later he was recaptured.

Going back to the escape bid that had ultimately resulted in Upham ending up at Colditz. The guard who was stationed in the tower with the machine gun, when Upham made his escape whilst exercising, later said that he didn't open fire on him, out of sheer respect and because he could see other German soldiers walking up the road towards where Upham was running and expected them to capture him.

Once at Colditz, the possibility of escaping was drastically reduced, and with the Allies sweeping across Europe at breakneck speed, Upham and his fellow prisoners quickly realised that their best option was to sit and wait until they were liberated. During the war, Colditz had witnessed a total of 186 escape attempts, 39 of which had been successful. Although it had been used by the Germans as a PoW camp since 7 November 1940, since May 1943 only British and American officers had been held there.

Upham joined them as he wanted to continue fighting the Germans, but he soon found himself back home in England, and by 20 June 1945, he was a married man, his new bride being Molly McTamney, and by September 1945 he had returned home to his native New Zealand.

On his return to New Zealand the sum of £10,000 was raised out of public subscriptions so that he could purchase a farm, but being the man he was, he turned down the kind offer, and instead the monies were donated to the C. H. Upham Scholarship Fund, which had been set up in his name for the exclusive use of children of ex-servicemen, so that they could afford to stay on at school for further education, and study at either Lincoln University or Canterbury College.

The farm idea was something which appealed to Upham, and so he obtained a New Zealand war rehabilitation loan and purchased a farm on Conway Flat, at Hundalee in North Canterbury. Despite his wartime injuries, Charles Upham went on to become a successful farmer. In his private life he and Molly were happily married and they brought up three daughters on the farm. In a somewhat surreal twist of fate, it turns out that Upham's wife Molly was a distant relative of Captain Noel Chavasse.

In January 1994, after nearly fifty years of farm life, Charles and Molly had to leave their lovely farm, and move to Christchurch because of his failing health. Charles Upham died on 22 November 1994. His funeral service took place at Christchurch Cathedral, and on the day thousands of well-wishers lined the streets of Christchurch to watch the funeral cortege pass by. After the ceremony he was buried in the graveyard at the St Paul's Church, Papanui. This was followed up with a memorial service that was held at St Martin-in-the-Fields church in the City of London the following year on 5 May. It was attended by members of the Royal Family, British and New Zealand government officials and military figures, past and present. It was a truly grand affair and a fitting send off to a truly great man.

Charles Upham's Victoria Cross and Bar were sold to the Imperial War Museum in London in November 2006, by his daughters, but due to New Zealand policy on the export from the country of items with such historic importance or value, Charles's medals were not allowed to leave the country, even for a location as prestigious as the Imperial War Museum. In the circumstances the medals were permanently loaned to the Waiouru Army Museum.

Chapter Eleven

John Wallace Linton

Although ten is an even number of entries to include in this book, having come to the end it is perhaps only fitting that one more entry is included.

John Wallace Linton was a proud Welshman born in Newport on 15 October 1905, a man's man who had the affectionate nickname of 'Tubby' due to his stout appearance, which he needed as a well-respected amateur Rugby player who was good enough to represent both the Royal Navy and the United Services.

He had enlisted in the Royal Navy in 1926 when he was 21, going on to work on submarines and was killed in action at La Maddalena Harbour in Italy on a date that has officially been recorded as 23 March 1943, by which time, besides the Victoria Cross, he had also been awarded the Distinguished Service Order, as well as the Distinguished Service Cross.

Whilst in the rank of acting sub lieutenant, he was promoted to the substantive rank of sub lieutenant, on 15 July 1926, and two years later to the very day, he was further promoted to lieutenant on 15 July 1928, with his seniority in rank adjusted accordingly. His suitability for further promotion having been recognised, he reached the rank of lieutenant commander on 1 July 1936.

Having volunteered for submarines, in 1940 he was commander of the Royal Navy submarine, HMS *Pandora* that was operating in the Far East, and saw her brought into Alexandria in May 1940, then on to Malta where she was destroyed in bombing attacks by the Luftwaffe on 1 April 1942.

By the time he was awarded the Victoria Cross he had already received two other military decorations.

On 6 May 1941, Lieutenant Commander John Wallace Linton of the Royal Navy submarine, HMS *Pandora* was awarded the Distinguished Service Cross: For courage and determination in sinking two Italian supply ships.

As was in keeping with the notification of such awards, news of it having being awarded was included in the edition of the *London Gazette* dated 2 May 1941.

On 15 September 1942, Commander John Wallace Linton, Distinguished Service Cross, was appointed a Companion of the Distinguished Service Order: For courage and skill in successful submarine patrols in HMS *Turbulent*. This appeared in the *London Gazette* on that date.

On 23 February 1943, the *Turbulent* sailed from Algiers to undertake a patrol in the Tyrrhenian Sea, an expanse of sea between mainland Italy and the islands of Sardinia and Sicily. It is known that nearly a week into the patrol the *Turbulent* took her first prize in the shape of the Italian steam ship, the *Vincenz*. On 11 March 1943 she attacked the Italian mail ship, the *Mafalda*. The next day, 12 March 1943, it was reported that the *Turbulent* was sailing close to the surface with her periscope up and part of the conning tower having breached the surface, as she scanned around looking for targets. She was spotted by the Italian anti-submarine trawler *Teti ll*. The outcome of that sighting is unclear, although after 12 March 1943, the *Turbulent* did not respond to any radio messages, and then failed to return to her base, as was expected on 23 March 1943. The actual date of her loss is not known, and the recorded date relates to when she should have returned to Algiers from her patrol.

Later research indicates that the incident on 12 March 1943 wasn't in fact the *Turbulent* at all, but the French submarine, the *Casablanca,* which survived the incident. It is known that throughout 1943, Royal Navy Lieutenant Keith Monin Stainton, and Royal Navy Signals expert, Charles William Beattie, both served on the *Casablanca*. Stainton worked as a liaison officer, and after the war he became the Conservative MP for Sudbury and Woodbridge between 1963 and 1983. Beattie's job was to safeguard and interpret secret cyphers that were sent to the submarine.

A possibility for the actual demise of the *Turbulent* is that she was attacked with depth charges by the Italian torpedo boat *Ardito*, off Punta Licosa, which is south of Naples. It is known that *Turbulent* was given orders to patrol off Bocca Piccola on 6 March 1943. On the same day, a combined convoy of Italian and German merchant ships sailed from Naples, escorted by a number of Italian torpedo boats.

In truth, it has not yet been fully determined who or what was responsible for the sinking of the *Turbulent* or where exactly it happened.

His posthumous award of the Victoria Cross was announced in the edition of the *London Gazette* dated 25 May 1943, for valour in command of HM Submarines. The citation of the award included the following:

> From the outbreak of War until HMS Turbulent's last patrol Commander Linton was constantly in command of submarines, and during that time inflicted great damage on the Enemy. He sank one Cruiser, one Destroyer, one U-boat, twenty-eight Supply Ships, some 100,000 tons in all, and destroyed three trains by gun-fire. In his last year he spent two hundred and fifty-four days at sea, submerged for nearly half the time, and his ship was hunted thirteen times and had two hundred and fifty depth charges aimed at her.
>
> His many and brilliant successes were due to his constant activity and skill, and the daring which never failed him when there was an Enemy to be attacked. On one occasion, for instance, in HMS *Turbulent*, he sighted a convoy of two Merchantmen and two Destroyers in mist and moonlight. He worked round ahead of the convoy and dived to attack it as it passed through the moon's rays. On bringing his sights to bear he found himself right ahead of a Destroyer. Yet he held his course till the Destroyer was almost on top of him, and, when his sights came on the convoy, he fired. His great courage and determination were rewarded. He sank one Merchantman and one Destroyer outright, and set the other Merchantman on fire so that she blew up.

The convoy attack mentioned in the above citation took place in the waters off Libya on 28 and 29 May 1942.

His career had been one of conspicuous gallantry and extreme devotion to duty in the presence of the enemy. A man who was constantly looking at ways of outwitting the enemy he found himself up against, whilst at the same time ensuring the safety of his crew.

Chapter Twelve

Victoria Cross Winners of the Second World War

Below is a list of the 181 men who were awarded the Victoria Cross during the course of the Second World War. Of these, 112 were dead by the end of the war. Some were killed in the incident that saw them awarded the Victoria Cross, whilst others were killed after receiving it.

The names are recorded below in alphabetical order rather than the date they were awarded.

Arthur **Aaron**. No. 218 Squadron, Royal Air Force.
Michael **Allmand**. 6th Queen Elizabeth's Own Ghurka Rifle.
Charles **Anderson**. 2nd/19th Battalion, Australian Imperial Army.
Eric **Anderson**. East Yorkshire Regiment.
John **Anderson**. Argyll and Sutherland Highlanders.
Richard **Annand**. Durham Light Infantry.
Cyril **Barton**. No. 578 Squadron, Royal Air Force.
John **Baskeyfield**. South Staffordshire Regiment.
Sidney **Bates**. Royal Norfolk Regiment.
Ian **Bazalgette**. No. 635 Squadron, Royal Air Force.
Stephen **Beattie**. HMS *Campbeltown*, Royal Navy.
John **Beeley**. King's Royal Rifle Corps.
Premindra **Bhagat**. Corps of Indian Engineers.
Frank **Blaker**. 9th Ghurka Rifles.
John **Brunt**. Sherwood Foresters.
Richard **Burton**. Duke of Wellington's (West Riding) Regiment
Robert **Cain**. South Staffordshire Regiment.
George **Cairns**. South Staffordshire Regiment.
Donald **Cameron**. HMS *X6* Royal Navy.
John **Campbell**. Royal Horse Artillery.

Kenneth **Campbell**. No. 22 Squadron, Royal Air Force.

Lorne **Campbell**. Argyll and Sutherland Highlanders.

Edward **Chapman**. Monmouthshire Regiment.

Edward **Charlton**. Irish Guards.

Leonard **Cheshire**. Royal Air Force.

Albert **Chowne**. 2nd/2nd Battalion, Australian Imperial Army

Aubrey **Cosens**. Queens Own Rifles of Canada.

John **Cruickshank**. No. 210 Squadron, Royal Air Force.

Arthur **Cumming**. Frontier Force Regiment.

David **Currie**. South Alberta Regiment.

Roden **Cutler**. Royal Australian Artillery.

Tom **Derrick**. 2nd/48th Battalion, Australian Imperial Force.

Fazal **Din**. 10th Baluch Regiment.

Dennis **Donnini**. Royal Scots Fusiliers.

Thomas **Durrant**. Corps of Royal Engineers.

George **Eardley**. King's Shropshire Light Infantry.

John **Edmondson**. 2nd/17th Battalion, Australian Imperial Force.

Hughie **Edwards**. No. 105 Squadron, Royal Air Force.

Keith **Elliott**. 22nd Battalion, New Zealand Expeditionary Force.

Harold **Ervine-Andrews**. East Lancashire Regiment.

Eugene **Esmonde**. No.825 Naval Air Squadron.

Edward **Fegen**. HMS *Jervis Bay,* Royal Navy.

Henry **Foote**. 7th Royal Tank Regiment.

John **Foote**. Royal Canadian Army Chaplain Corps.

Ian **Fraser**. HMS *XE3* Royal Navy.

John **French**. 2nd/9th Australian Imperial Force.

Christopher **Furness**. Welsh Guards.

Philip **Gardner**. 4th Royal Tank Regiment.

Donald **Garland**. No. 12 Squadron, Royal Air Force.

Yeshwant **Ghadge**. Maratha Light Infantry.

Gaje **Ghale**. 5th Gurkha Rifles.

Guy **Gibson**. No. 617 Squadron, Royal Air Force.

James **Gordon**. 2nd/31st Battalion, Australian Imperial Force.

Thomas **Gould**. HMS *Thrasher*, Royal Navy.

Percival **Gratwick**. 2nd/48th Battalion, Australian Imperial Force.

Robert **Gray**. HMS *Formidable*, Royal Navy.

Thomas **Gray**. No. 12 Squadron, Royal Air Force.

John **Grayburn**. Parachute Regiment.

George **Gristock**. Royal Norfolk Regiment.
George **Gunn**. 3rd Regiment Royal Horse Artillery.
Arthur **Gurney**. 2nd/48th Battalion, Australian Imperial Force.
Bhanbhagta **Gurung**. 2nd Gurkha Rifles.
Lachhiman **Gurung**. 8th Gurkha Rifles.
Thaman **Gurung**. 5th Gurkha Rifles.
Abdul **Hafiz**. 9th Jat Infantry.
Ali **Haidar**. 13th Frontier Force Rifles.
John **Hannah**. No. 83 Squadron, Royal Air Force.
Eric **Harden**. Royal Army Medical Corps.
John **Harman**. Queens Own Royal West Kent Regiment.
John **Harper**. York & Lancaster Regiment.
Jack **Hinton**. 2nd Division, New Zealand Expeditionary Force.
Charles **Hoey**. Lincolnshire Regiment.
Stanley **Hollis**. Green Howards.
David **Hornell**. No. 162 Squadron. Royal Canadian Air Force.
Alec **Horwood**. Queens Royal Regiment (West Surrey).
Clive **Hulme**. 2nd Division, New Zealand Expeditionary Force.
Thomas **Hunter**. 43 Commando Royal Marines.
James **Jackman**. Royal Northumberland Fusiliers.
Norman **Jackson**. No. 106 Squadron, Royal Air Force.
Namdeo **Jadav**. Maratha Light Infantry.
David **Jamieson**. Royal Norfolk Regiment.
Francis **Jefferson**. Lancashire Regiment.
Karamjeet **Judge**. 15th Punjab Regiment.
Richard **Kelliher**. 2nd/25th Battalion, Australian Imperial Force.
Edward **Kenna**. 2nd/4th Battalion, Australian Imperial Force.
John **Kenneally**. Irish Guards.
Geoffrey **Keyes**. No. 11 Scottish Commando.
William **Kibby**. 2nd/48th Australian Imperial Force.
Bruce **Kingsbury**. 2nd/14th Australian Imperial Force.
George **Knowland**. No. 1 Commando.
Ganju **Lama**. 7th Gurkha Rifles.
Anders **Lassen**. Special Air Service.
Herbert **Le Patourel**. Hampshire Regiment.
Nigel **Leakey**. King's African Rifles.
Roderick **Learoyd**. No. 49 Squadron, Royal Air Force.
Ian **Liddell**. Coldstream Guards.

John **Linton**. HMS *Turbulent,* Royal Navy.

David **Lord**. No. 271 Squadron, Royal Air Force.

Charles **Lyell**. Scots Guards.

John **Mackey**. 2nd/3rd Pioneer Battalion, Australian Imperial Force.

John **Mahony**. Westminster Regiment.

Hugh **Malcolm**. No. 18 Squadron, Royal Air Force.

James **Mangennis**. HMS *XE3*, Royal Navy.

Leslie **Manser**. No. 50 Squadron, Royal Air Force.

Jack **Mantle**. HMS *Foylebank.* Royal Navy.

Charles **Merritt**. South Saskatchewan Regiment

Ron **Middleton**. No. 149 Squadron, Royal Air Force.

Anthony **Miers**. HMS *Torbay*, Royal Navy.

George **Mitchell**. London Scottish.

Andrew **Mynarski**. No. 419 Squadron, Royal Canadian Air Force.

Moana-Nui-a-Kiwa **Nagarini**. 28th Maori Battalion, New Zealand
    Expeditionary Force.

John **Nettleton**. No. 44 Squadron, Royal Air Force.

Augustus **Newman**. Essex Regiment.

William **Newton**. No. 22 Squadron, Royal Australian Air Force.

Harry **Nicholls**. Grenadier Guards.

Eric **Nicolson**. No. 249 Squadron, Royal Air Force.

Gerard **Norton**. Kaffrarian Rifles.

John **Osborn**. Winnipeg Grenadiers.

Robert **Palmer**. No. 109 Squadron, Royal Air Force.

Frank **Partridge**. 8th Battalion, Australian Imperial Force.

Frederick **Peters**. HMS *Walney,* Royal Navy.

Basil **Place**. HMS *X7*, Royal Navy.

Patrick **Porteous**. Royal Regiment of Artillery.

Tul **Pun**. 6th Gurkha Rifles.

Lionel **Queripel**. Parachute Regiment.

Agansing **Rai**. 5th Gurkha Rifles.

Bhandari **Ram**. 10th Baluch Regiment.

Chhelu **Ram**. 6th Rajputana Rifles.

Kamal **Ram**. 8th Punjab Rifles.

Richhpal **Ram**. 6th Rajputana Rifles.

John **Randle**. Royal Norfolk Regiment.

Reginald **Rattey**. 25th Battalion, Australian Imperial Force.

Claud **Raymond**. Corps of Royal Engineers.

William **Reid**. No. 61 Squadron, Royal Air Force.

Peter **Roberts**. HMS *Thrasher,* Royal Navy.

Maurice **Rogers**. Wiltshire Regiment.

Gerard **Roope**. HMS *Glowworm,* Royal Navy.

Robert **Ryder**. HMS *Campbeltown*, Royal Navy.

Willward **Sandys-Clarke**. Loyal Regiment (North Lancashire)

William **Savage**. HM Motor Gun Boat, Royal Navy.

Arthur **Scarf**. No. 62 Squadron, Royal Air Force.

Derek **Seagrim**. Green Howards.

Alfred **Sephton**. HMS *Coventry*, Royal Navy.

Sher **Shah**. 16th Punjab Regiment.

Robert **Sherbrooke**. HMS *Onslow*, Royal Navy.

William **Sidney**. Grenadier Guards.

Gian **Singh**. 15th Punjab Regiment.

Nand **Singh**. Sikh Regiment.

Prakash **Singh**. 8th Punjab Regiment.

Ram **Singh,** 1st Punjab Regiment.

Umrao **Singh**. 81st West African Division.

Prakash **Singh-Chib**. 13th Frontier Force Rifles.

Ernest **Smith**. Seaforth Highlanders of Canada.

Quentin **Smythe**. Royal Natal Carabineers.

Richard **Stannard**. HMT *Arab*, Royal Navy.

Leslie **Starcevich**. 2nd/43rd Battalion, Australian Imperial Force.

James **Stokes**. King's Shropshire Light Infantry.

Sefanaia **Sukanaivalu**. Fiji Infantry Regiment.

Edwin **Swales**. No. 582 Squadron. Royal Air Force.

Lalbahadur **Thapa**. 2nd Gurkha Rifles.

Netrabahadur **Thapa**. 5th Gurkha Rifles.

Sher **Thapa**. 9th Ghurkha Rifles.

George **Thompson**. No. 9 Squadron, Royal Air Force.

Frederick **Tilston**. Essex Scottish Regiment.

Frederick George **Topham**. 1st Canadian Parachute Battalion.

Leonard **Trent**. No. 487 Squadron, Royal New Zealand Air Force.

Lloyd **Trigg**. No. 200 Squadron, Royal Air Force.

Paul **Triquet**. Royal 22nd Regiment.

Hanson **Turner**. West Yorkshire Regiment (The Prince of Wales Own).

Victor **Turner**. Rifle Brigade (Prince Consort's Own).

Charles **Upham**. 2nd Division, New Zealand Expeditionary Force.
Richard **Wakeford**. Hampshire Regiment.
Adam **Wakenshaw**. Durham Light Infantry.
Malcolm **Wanklyn**. HMS *Upholder*, Royal Navy.
Bernard **Warburton-Lee**. HMS *Hardy*, Royal Navy.
James **Ward**. No. 75 Squadron, Royal Air Force.
Tasker **Watkins**. Welch Regiment.
Basil **Weston**. Green Howards.
Thomas **Wilkinson**. HMS *Li Wo*.
Eric **Wilson**. East Surrey Regiment.
Peter **Wright**. Coldstream Guards.

The first Victoria Cross to be awarded in the Second World War was for an action that took place on 10 April 1940, involving Captain Bernard Armitage Warburton-Lee, a Welshman, born in Wrexham on 13 September 1895, who although having enlisted in the Royal Navy in 1908, did not serve during the First World War.

He attended the British army's Staff College at Camberley, Surrey between 1931 and 1932, and in 1936, during the Spanish Civil War, he was the captain of HMS *Witch,* sent by the Foreign Office to the naval station at Ferrol in North Western Spain to pick up British civilians, due to the fear of social unrest. Having successfully completed his mission, he sailed for Britain from Spain on 22 July 1936.

During the Second World War the following incident took place which saw Captain Bernard Warburton-Lee awarded the Victoria Cross.

On 10 April 1940 at Ofotfjord, Narvik, in Norway, during the First Battle of Narvik, Warburton-Lee commanded the 2nd Destroyer Flotilla, which consisted of five destroyers of the Royal Navy: HMS *Hardy, Havock, Hostile, Hotspur and Hunter.* On board HMS *Hardy*, Warburton-Lee carried out a surprise and successful attack on a number of German destroyers and merchant vessels during a severe snowstorm. Almost immediately afterwards Warburton-Lee and his flotilla found themselves engaging with five more German destroyers and during this engagement, Warburton-Lee was mortally wounded when a shell fired from one of the German destroyers struck the bridge of HMS *Hardy.* For his actions during this engagement he was posthumously awarded the Victoria Cross.

The citation for his award included the following:

> For gallantry, enterprising and daring in command of the force engaged in the First Battle of Narvik, on 10th April, 1940. On being ordered to carry out an attack on Narvik, Captain Warburton-Lee learned that the enemy was holding the place in much greater force than had been thought. He signalled to the Admiralty that six German destroyers and one submarine were there, that the channel might be mined, and that he intended to attack at dawn. The Admiralty replied that he alone could judge whether to attack, and that whatever decision he made would have full support. Captain Warburton-Lee led his flotilla of five destroyers up the fjord in heavy snow-storms, arriving off Narvik just after daybreak. He took the enemy completely by surprise and made three successful attacks on warships and merchantmen in the harbour. As the flotilla withdrew, five enemy destroyers of superior gun power were encountered and engaged. The Captain was mortally wounded by a shell which hit the bridge of HMS Hardy. His last signal was 'continue to engage the enemy'.

Captain Warburton-Lee was also awarded the Norwegian War Cross and was also mentioned in despatches. His body was recovered and buried at the Ballangen New Cemetery, which is situated about 25km south-west of Narvick.

The last Victoria Cross of the Second World War was awarded to Canadian Lieutenant Robert Hampton Gray, who at the time was serving as a pilot with No. 1841 Squadron, based on HMS *Formidable*.

Gray had enlisted in the Royal Canadian Naval Volunteer Reserve at HMCS *Tecumseh*, in Calgary, Alberta, in 1940. His initial assignment, once he arrived in England, was with No. 757 Squadron at Winchester.

In April 1945, HMS *Formidable* joined the British Pacific Fleet, which took part in the Battle of Okinawa, and had been tasked with neutralising the Japanese airfields in the Sakishima Islands, which it did between 26 March and 10 April 1945.

On 24 July 1945, Gray led an attack which resulted in the damaging of a Japanese merchant vessel, along with two seaplane bases and an air base, Four days later he helped in the destruction of a Japanese destroyer in the seas off Tokyo. This saw his actions rewarded with a Distinguished Service Order, the citation of which appeared in the *London Gazette* on 21 August 1945, by which time he was already dead.

On 9 August 1945, Gray, flying a Vought F4U Corsair aircraft, led an attack on a group of Japanese naval vessels at Onagawa Bay, Miyagi Prefecture in Japan. This resulted in one of the Japanese ships, the Etorofu-class escort ship, the *Amakusa*, being sunk, after which his aircraft crashed into the sea. Gray's body was never recovered. For this action, Gray was awarded the Victoria Cross, the citation of which appeared in the *London Gazette* on 13 November 1945. It read as follows:

> The King has been graciously pleased to approve the award of the Victory Cross for valour to the late Temporary Lieutenant, Robert Hampton Gray, Royal Canadian Naval Volunteer Reserve, for great valour in leading an attack on a Japanese destroyer in Onagawa Wan, on 9 August 1945. In the face of fire from shore batteries and a heavy concentration of fire from some five warships, Lieutenant Gray pressed home his attack, flying very low in order to ensure success, and, although he was hit and his aircraft was in flames, he obtained at least one direct hit, sinking the destroyer. Lieutenant Gray has consistently shown a brilliant fighting spirit and most inspiring leadership.

Gray was the last Canadian to be awarded the Victoria Cross.

During the war, twenty-three Victoria Crosses were awarded to members of the Royal Navy or the Royal Naval Volunteer Reserve, twenty-nine to members of the Royal Air Force, the Royal Australian Air Force, the Royal Canadian Air Force, or the Royal New Zealand Air Force. The remaining 129 were soldiers.

Those who were awarded the Victoria Crosses came from a number of different countries including: Australia, Canada, England, Fiji, India, Ireland, Scotland, Wales, Nepal, New Zealand, Pakistan, and South Africa.

In Closing

I hope you have enjoyed the book and my interpretation of the top ten recipients of the Victoria Cross from the period of the Second World War. As I have already said, I mean no offence or disrespect to anybody who was awarded the Victoria Cross, who is still alive, and who is not in my top ten. It is after all, only my opinion. Some people will agree with some or all of the names I have chosen and there will be some who will disagree.

Anybody who has been awarded the Victoria Cross is an extremely brave individual, and does not require my endorsement to confirm their heroic and well-deserved status.

Having read through all the citations for the 182 Victoria Crosses that were awarded during the Second World War, I have named my top ten with the reasons why. Although not an easy task, it was a very enjoyable one.

There are so many words that could be used to describe these men and their individual acts that saw them awarded their Victoria Crosses, but one thing that many of them had in common was that before the war, they were just ordinary men. But when the fighting began, they stepped up to the plate, and found it within themselves to carry out remarkable acts of gallantry and bravery, in the most difficult and sometimes the most dangerous of circumstances. The fact they carried out such acts in the first place is a testimony to their bravery, but the fact that by doing what they did – more often than not putting their own lives at risk whilst attempting to save others – marks them with a greatness that very few ever achieve in life.

I have had the pleasure of meeting and interviewing a man who was awarded the Victoria Cross, not during the Second World War, but the Korean War. I met Bill Speakman in April 2017. At the time he was an

In Pensioner at the Royal Hospital Chelsea, and I had visited him to interview him for a future book about the four Victoria Crosses awarded during the Korean War. At the time Bill was the only one of the four still alive, as two of the awards had been given posthumously and the third recipient had died in 1986. Sadly, Bill subsequently passed away on 20 June 2018.

Bill was a very interesting character. I met him when he was 89 years old and he still had an edge about him, even then. A tall man, about 6ft 5ins in height with a very strong northern accent. A gentle giant by all accounts in his day, but still not the type of man to rile for no particular reason. I am not easily scared, but there was something about him that told me that he would not have been a man to mess with!

We spoke for about an hour and he told me about how he came to join the army in 1945, but too late to be a part of the Second World War, and his time spent in the SAS, which he joined in 1953 and served with during the Malayan Emergency. He made mention of liking the odd drink or two, and a couple of bar-room brawls that he 'may or may not have been involved in'. He smiled when he recalled how many times he had lost his 'stripes', due in the main to bar-room brawls. Talking about MPs, military policemen that is, not members of parliament, 'They used to look for me, and then try and wind me up, just because they knew I had a VC,' he said with a knowing smile. 'But I won more of those scraps than I lost. I suppose it made them feel good about themselves, nicking somebody like me.' Bill added that he didn't go looking for trouble, but that it quite often found him, usually after he had been in the jungles of Malaya for a few months at a time when he was in the SAS. 'I enjoyed a beer or two in the bars of Singapore after returning from a stint in the jungle, who wouldn't?'

But when it got round to talking about what he did to earn his Victoria Cross, he simply minimalised what he had done to: 'I was on this hill with my mates, and the Chinese were trying to kill us, and I for one didn't want to die, so I had to do what I had to do to stay alive. I was just doing my job, what I was trained to do. That was it really. Nothing special, and it wasn't just me,' he said modestly. The reality of what actually happened, was somewhat different.

The citation for the award of his Victoria Cross, which he had framed and hanging on the wall of his room at the Royal Hospital Chelsea, reads as follows:

The King has been graciously pleased to approve the award of the Victoria Cross to:

14471590 Private William Speakman, Black Watch (Royal Highland Regiment), attached to the 1st Battalion, The King's Own Scottish Borderers, in recognition of gallant and distinguished services in Korea.

From 0400 hours, 4th November 1951, the defensive positions held by the 1st Battalion, The King's Own Scottish Borderers, were continuously subjected to heavy and accurate enemy shell and mortar fire. At 1545 hours this fire became intense and continued thus for the next two hours, considerably damaging the defences and wounding a number of men.

At 1645 hours, the enemy in their hundreds advanced in wave upon wave against the King's Own Scottish Borderers' positions, and by 1745 hours fierce hand to hand fighting was taking place on every position.

Private Speakman, a member of B Company, Headquarters, learning the section holding the left shoulder of the Company's position had been seriously depleted by casualties, had had its NCOs wounded and was being overrun, decided on his own initiative to drive the enemy off the position and keep them off it. To effect this he collected quickly a large pile of grenades and a party of six men. Then displaying complete disregard for his own personal safety, he led his party in a series of grenade charges against the enemy; and continued doing so as each successive wave of enemy reached the crest of the hill. The force and determination of his charges broke up each successive enemy onslaught and resulted in an ever growing pile of enemy dead.

Having led some ten charges, through withering enemy machine gun and mortar fire, Private Speakman was eventually severely wounded in the leg. Undaunted by his wounds, he continued to lead charge after charge against the enemy and it was only after a direct order from his superior officer that he agreed to pause for a first field dressing to be applied to his wounds. Having had his wounds bandaged, Private Speakman immediately re-joined his comrades and led them again and again forward in a series of grenade charges, up to the time of withdrawal of his company at 2100 hours.

At the critical moment of the withdrawal, amidst an inferno of enemy machine gun and mortar fire, as well as grenades, Private Speakman led a final charge to clear the crest of the hill and hold it, whilst the remainder of his Company withdrew. Encouraging his gallant, but now sadly depleted party, he assailed the enemy with showers of grenades and kept them at bay sufficiently long for his Company to effect its withdrawal.

Under the stress and strain of this battle, Private Speakman's outstanding powers of leadership were revealed and he so dominated the situation, that he inspired his comrades to stand firm and fight the enemy to a standstill.

His great gallantry and utter contempt for his own personal safety were an inspiration to all his comrades. He was by his heroic actions, personally responsible for causing enormous losses to the enemy, assisting his Company to maintain their position for some four hours and saving the lives of many of his comrades when they were forced to withdraw from their position.

Private Speakman's heroism under intense fire throughout the operation and when painfully wounded was beyond praise and is deserving of supreme recognition.

Bill Speakman is believed to have personally killed more than 300 enemy soldiers, simply because he wanted to stay alive and save the lives of his comrades.

Bill Speakman's award of the Victoria Cross was also somewhat unique, as he was awarded it by King George VI, on 28 December 1951, but after the king died on 6 February 1952, Speakman became the first person invested with the Victoria Cross by Queen Elizabeth II.

No one is suggesting for one second that every holder of the Victoria Cross is or was cut from the same cloth as Bill Speakman, or came from the same social background for that matter, but what they did have in common was their ethos of dedication and devotion to duty, a determination to get the job done, even if it meant putting their own lives at risk, and a desire to put their colleagues before themselves.

For every man who has ever been awarded a Victoria Cross, they were not seeking fame and glory, they simply wanted to right a wrong. They were exercising their inbuilt desire to act to protect others, which for them was second nature. To the rest of us, soldiers or civilians alike, it matters not, it goes to show what is achievable if a man has the ability to find within himself the mental strength to overcome his inner fears, for the greater good.

There were many others who carried out acts of bravery during the course of the Second World War, who received lesser awards than the Victoria Cross, there were others who undoubtedly should have been awarded the Victoria Cross, but because of the circumstances that they found themselves in, there was nobody left alive who had witnessed the events who could nominate them for the award.

The standard and level of bravery required to be awarded a Victoria Cross is so high that only fifteen have been awarded since the end of the Second World War. This has included the Korean War, the troubles in Northern Ireland, as well as the Falklands War, the first and second Gulf Wars, the war in Iraq, the war in Afghanistan, and numerous other occasions where Special Forces operatives have been deployed around the world.

There are currently just nine living recipients of the Victoria Cross, the last five of which were awarded for actions in Afghanistan between 2007 and 2015.

At the time of writing this book (2019) the oldest living recipient of the Victoria Cross is John Alexander Cruickshank, who was born on 20 May 1920, in Aberdeen, Scotland, and who was awarded his medal in 1944, whilst serving as a Flying Officer in the Royal Air Force, with No. 210 Squadron in the Atlantic Ocean.

Next in line is Rambahadur Limbu, who was born in Nepal on 8 July 1939. He was a lance corporal serving with the 2nd Battalion, 10th Princess Mary's Own Gurkha Rifles, when he was awarded his Victoria Cross in 1966, for actions during the Malaya Emergency the previous year.

IN CLOSING

Keith Payne was born in Queensland, Australia on 30 August 1933. He was awarded his Victoria Cross in 1969, whilst serving as a Warrant Officer Class II with the Australian Army Training Team in Vietnam, during the Vietnam War.

Johnson Beharry was born in Grenada on 26 July 1979 and was serving as a private with the 1st Battalion, The Princess of Wales's Royal Regiment in Iraq in 2005, when he was awarded his Victoria Cross.

Bill Henry 'Willie' Apiata was born in New Zealand on 28 June 1972, and was serving as a corporal in the New Zealand Special Air Service, when he was awarded his Victoria Cross (for New Zealand) in 2007 for an action in Afghanistan in 2004.

Mark Donaldson was born in Waratah, Australia on 2 April 1979, and was serving as a trooper in the Australian Special Air Service Regiment, when he was awarded the Victoria Cross (for Australia) in 2009 for service in Afghanistan during 2008.

Ben Roberts-Smith was born in Perth, Australia on 1 November 1978, and was serving as a corporal in the Australian Special Air Service Regiment, when he was awarded the Victoria Cross (for Australia) in 2011 for service in Afghanistan during 2010.

Daniel Alan Keighran was born in Queensland, Australia on 18 June 1983, and was serving as a corporal with the 6th Battalion, Royal Australian Regiment, when he was awarded the Victoria Cross (for Australia) in 2012 for service in Afghanistan during 2010.

Joshua Leakey was born in Horsham in Sussex in 1988, and was awarded his Victoria Cross for action he displayed whilst serving as a lance corporal with the 1st Battalion, Parachute Regiment in Afghanistan in 2013. He was presented with his medal in 2015. He was the only British soldier to be awarded the Victoria Cross non-posthumously during the war in Afghanistan, and he is also the only current living English recipient of the Victoria Cross.

On 19 May 1941, during the Second World War, a relative of Joshua's, Nigel Leakey, a second cousin, twice removed, was involved in an action in Kolito, Abyssinia, whilst fighting the Italians. He was killed in the action, and was posthumously awarded the Victoria Cross.

Thankfully, others will follow in their footsteps over the course of time.

Index

Sources

www.britishnewspaperarchive.co.uk
www.victoriacross.org.uk
www.adb.anu.edu.au
www.vconline.org.uk
www.cwgc.org
www.ancestry.co.uk
www.blaydonwinlatonwarmemorialproject.btck.co.uk
www.thebetterwiki.com
www.bradfordbrothersofwittonpark.org.uk
www.manfamily.org
www.commandoveterans.org
www.uboat.net
www.vconline.org.uk
www.historypress.co.uk

About the Author

Stephen is a happily retired police officer having served with Essex Police as a constable for thirty years between 1983 and 2013. He is married to Tanya who is also his best friend.

Both his sons, Luke and Ross, were members of the armed forces, collectively serving five tours of Afghanistan between 2008 and 2013. Both were injured on their first tour. This led to Stephen's first book: *Two Sons in a Warzone – Afghanistan: The True Story of a Fathers Conflict,* which was published in October 2010.

Both of his grandfathers served in and survived the First World War, one with the Royal Irish Rifles, the other in the Mercantile Navy, whilst his father was a member of the Royal Army Ordnance Corps during the Second World War.

Stephen collaborated with one of his writing partners, Ken Porter, on a previous book published in August 2012, *German PoW Camp 266 – Langdon Hills,* which spent six weeks as the number one best-selling book in Waterstones, Basildon between March and April 2013. Steve and Ken collaborated on a further four books in the Towns & Cities in the Great War series by Pen and Sword. Stephen has also written other titles in the same series of books, and in February 2017 his book, *The Surrender of Singapore – Three Years of Hell 1942-45,* was published. This was followed in March 2018 by *Against All Odds: Walter Tull the Black Lieutenant,* and in January 2019, *A History of the Royal Hospital Chelsea – 1682-2017 – The Warriors Repose,* which he wrote with his wife, Tanya. They have also written two other books together.

Stephen has also co-written three crime thrillers which were published between 2010 and 2012, which centre round a fictional detective, named Terry Danvers.

When not writing, Tanya and Stephen enjoy the simplicity of walking their three German shepherd dogs early each morning, at a time when most sensible people are still fast asleep in their beds.